PORCELAIN SOUL

By

ANDREEA LICHI

Scotland Street Press
EDINBURGH

First Published in the UK in 2022 by

Scotland Street Press

100 Willowbrae Avenue

Edinburgh EH8 7HU

A CIP record for this book is available from the British Library.

ISBN 978-1-910895-61-0

Translated from Romanian by Gabriela Achihai, Julia Smyth and Scotland Street Press

Typeset and cover design by Antonia Shack, Edinburgh

Cover artwork ©Isabelle Weir

Printed and bound by Clays Ltd.

For those who believe that there is no way back

Author's note

I chose to lay down these lines because my soul was supersaturated. I can't call myself a writer, I'm just a storyteller. A storyteller who has written down her feelings over the last six years out of necessity. I needed to get rid of some of the emotions that weighed on me every day. I also chose to write because when suffering hit me it would have been good for me to read a similar story. Maybe then, I would not have felt like the only damaged person in the world. Maybe these words will help someone someday. They are not big words, because I couldn't think of metaphors when I looked through my life. These are simple words, said with all my heart. Reader, if you reach the last page, I hope you will understand how fragile you are, but also how lucky, because you can see the words and actually feel the texture of the pages that your fingers touch.

Contents

Prologue

It is past the middle of July. In less than three weeks I will turn fourteen. For my birthday I should have gone to France, to Paris with the folk dancing ensemble I am part of, or rather which I was part of. I was supposed to stay there eighteen days. The first six to seven would have been visiting the countries on the way to France, and the remainder staying with a French family, who would have walked me round the streets of Paris, just like when I stayed with a family in Istanbul last year. My friends and I would have ended each day with traditional Moldovan singing and dancing, on the festival stages prepared for us. What a beautiful gift that would have been!

It's extremely hot outside, or at least that is how it seems. As proof, even the chocolate bar which Vali brought me, and has been left next to my bed, seems to have melted.

'Daddy, can you turn on the air conditioning?'

'Of course, but only for ten minutes. We have to go to Mr Adi.'

I keep looking in the mirror, trying to recognise myself, but with each passing day I look worse and worse. I can't see anything of myself, the person I was four months ago. The huge black wheelchair takes up the whole mirror. In the middle, I can see a soul of about forty-eight kilograms, 1.7m tall, wearing a pink blouse – which is a bit big for me, but like that so they can dress me – blue three-quarter length trousers and black sneakers.

The day has not started well. First my butterfly needle got clogged in less than twelve hours. Then it took over an hour to insert a new needle, because my hands and my feet have been ruined by the hundreds of needles poked into my veins. Worst of all, I had to say goodbye to my beautiful hair. As if it's not enough to have bald patches all over my head, I had to have my hair shaved at the back. It had matted itself into a ball from always lying on my back, and not being able to sit up for my mother to comb it. I used to have very long hair down to my bum and I cared about it a lot. Now, I'm completely bald at the back, with just enough hair at the front to look like a girl.

'Andreea, we should go.' My father comes towards me about to unlock my chair.

'Please, two more minutes!' I plead. 'Mother should be back soon from the shop, I asked her to buy me some sweets and I would like to eat one before going to Mr Adi's.'

'Just two minutes, I mean it. Two minutes and we are leaving,' my father insists.

I nod and stare at my reflection in the mirror. I look at the big, full-on scars which I must get used to, because I will wear them all my life. A life which will not be very long if my blood tests do not return to normal and if the fever, caused by the bad urinary tract infection, does not go away.

I stare at my middle fingers on my left hand, the fingers don't look like fingers, more like swellings lined with horrible scars, which continue to the wrist joint. Then, I look up and see the huge scar, about ten centimetres long, on the right side of my neck. My soul hurts and I want to scream. I want to scream so loudly that all the people who hurt me can hear, especially the boy who caused me to end up like this, but I can speak no more on pain, so I remain silent and look at a tear that has appeared and runs down my cheek. One tear. Another tear besides the millions of tears I shed for that day, for that moment, for that second that triggered hell in my life. That second when my brain was absent. Part of me died then, but another part remained, to cause pain, to torment and to shed tears.

1

The day it all changed

Thursday, 27th March 2014

It's six a.m. and my phone alarm is going off, as it does every day of the week. I turn it off and get out of bed quickly, faster than I usually do. I get dressed in my favourite blue jeans, which I bought last month, a white T-shirt dotted with a few gold pearls around the neckline, a black shirt, unbuttoned and tied at the bottom around my hips. I also put on the bracelets I love, my necklace with a blue ball and my favourite gold star earrings, given to me by my Turkish family last year when I stayed with them. I can't go out without a little foundation and mascara and by the time I leave the bathroom, my father has his jacket on.

'Have a great day at work, Daddy!' I say with a wide smile.

'Thank you very much, and you,' he replies, then sets off to work.

It's almost quarter to seven. I can't believe I moved so fast. I must admit, I'm usually lazy in the morning. I put my shoes on and check my bag again, it may be the tenth time I have done it, but I'm always careful not to forget anything and I think that's a good thing.

'Mum, I'm leaving, have a nice day at work!' I shout from the hall.

'Already?' she says, barely awake.

'Yes, it's almost seven, you should get up.'

'Okay, okay. You usually leave after seven.'

'I was faster today. Have a nice day!'

'Same to you.'

I step outside. Magda has just arrived.

'Good morning, sunshine,' she says, full of smiles.

'Morning to you too, honey! I'm glad you're better today!'

Magda's grandfather from Botoşani died last week and she only returned home last night. I talked to her on the phone while she was gone, and I felt the pain in her voice. It's damn hard when you lose a loved one, although sooner or later we all go through it. And then one day it will be my turn, and yours, and everyone's turn to be the ones to leave. This is the thing we call life. This is the creation of the bearded man from above. We are born, we grow, we explore, and we get educated. Then we make friends and experience the most beautiful feelings, we get married, we plant hearts, we raise them. We try to install in them the best version of ourselves, the highest hopes and the highest principles.

But all the while we are still suffering. Some less, some more, some too much. In any case, we all suffer. We all have something that grinds us, presses us, hurts us, damages us, stings us, burns us, ends us slowly, but surely. Though, to be honest, I think that without suffering, life would be too boring and meaningless, it would not make sense – of course, everything in moderation! But if it were not for suffering, we would not really learn how to cherish our loved ones, and especially how to cherish this gift from God: life.

Sometimes we need a cold shower to steer us, to show us how important little things are, how important it is to touch a loved one, how wonderful it is that we can move, that we feel, see, hear, and interact – ultimately, how important it is that we live. These things may seem small, but they are the most important things, we may only end up seeing this when our lives are out of control.

But when we die and pass over, these things leave deep traces in the souls of loved ones.

Today I am supposed to be at school celebrating our headmistress's birthday, but Magda has asked me to go with her to meet Alex, the boy she has been texting. I chose to go with her knowing that I would not miss too much at school by skipping the day, especially since 'Special Week' was approaching. Sure, there were still things to discuss about the activities scheduled for that, especially to do with the long-awaited paragliding jump but I was already looking forward to the week, because every outing with our class was phenomenal. This is not only because we, the students of the seventh grade B team, are the 'coolest ladybugs' – as the headmistress liked to tell us – but also because our teacher is the most super-mega-cool teacher.

'And … how are you today?' I asked Magda as we made our way to the bus station.

'I'm better, I got used to the idea … didn't you say that we all die one day and that we can't escape it? That is, there is nothing I can do to bring him back. Shall we go downtown?'

'Well, where did you say we should all meet up?'

'Ecstasy, that's what the cafe is called. Alex said it was close to the Catholic cathedral, near that passage from the centre.'

'We can get there by the Church or by the Economic high school. Let's go by Economic.'

'Good. By the way, he also said that he was bringing his friend along.'

'Ok.'

'Thank you for coming with me and for always being so close to me.'

'That's what your best friend is for, right?'

'Hug?'

'Hug!'

We hugged and got on the bus. Amazingly there were some empty seats, so we sat down. The bus was unnaturally empty for seven-thirty, when we usually had to stand up. Maybe everyone had begun to smell the Easter holiday, or maybe the spring air makes the students skip school. Even the old women were missing from the bus. They were usually the first on, to get to the market to make sure they didn't miss the freshest fruit and vegetables.

'Why are you laughing?' I ask Magda.

'I was thinking...'

'What? Tell me, girl, let me laugh too!'

'Isn't Alex cute?'

'What sort of question is that?' I start to laugh.

'Well, isn't he? Come on, Andreea, say something!'

'Girl, I don't know. He's not my type. And I don't even know him. You talked to him, not me!'

'Okay... I just wanted an opinion from my best friend, but I see you have nothing to say.'

'He is not my type!' I say in her ear, laughing.

'It's typical that you only like guys with blue eyes, are the others not good enough? she replied tensely.

'Magda don't take it badly! We are all different. I have some principles, you have others. I like one kind of boy, you like another. We are unique. It's you who needs to like him, not me. Anyway, you're the older one and you should know that. It's not like this is the first time you've met.'

'Good, good. Don't get upset now.'

'Look, I'll talk to him, and then I'll tell you my general opinion, so you can get a good night's sleep. And now, let's get off.'

We had talked all the way and time passed very quickly. In less than fifteen minutes we reached the Economic high school. It was hot outside, maybe too hot for a late March morning. In fact, the whole month was very warm and beautiful.

'I've got a message. He says they are at the café.'

'Okay, tell him we'll be there in ten minutes.'

We were still a little way from the café, but luckily for us, we found it quickly. I had been through that area dozens of times, but I had no idea the café existed. Opposite is a very good pretzel shop which I used to buy pretzels from. We went into Ecstasy, Magda first. The boys were playing pool. They saw us, left the cues on the table and came towards us.

'It looks like you found us,' Alex said.

'Hey, of course, we're smart girls!' said Magda, smiling.

'This is Cătălin, my friend,' Alex introduced the boy standing behind him.

'Magda, nice to meet you.' They shook hands formally. 'This is Andreea, my best friend.'

After I was introduced to the two of them, we sat down at a table and they started talking. Alex and Magda had a lot of talking to do. I had no idea what they were talking about, their voices blurred into the background, I tapped on my phone with one hand while stirring my cappuccino cup with the other.

'Andreea ...'

'Yes?'

'Magda and I have been the only ones talking, tell us something about yourself,' said Alex.

'What would you like to know?'

'Anything.'

'Well .... I study at Alecsandri High School. I am thirteen. I'm in the seventh grade. I dance in a group of folk dancers. I love travelling. Blue is my favourite colour, and... I can't think of anything else, ask me again!'

'I don't believe you! Are you really thirteen?' asked Alex and Cătălin in astonishment.

'Yes, I know I look older, but yes, I'm thirteen, but I turn fourteen in less than five months.

'Ahh, so you're almost fourteen.'

'Yeah, I thought Magda told you about me. She usually does. Sometimes I don't even know what she's said.'

'No, she didn't really tell me anything about you. She just told me you were coming too and gave me your Facebook,' Alex continued in a serious tone.

'Great. Nice phone! Can I see it?' I said, changing topic.

'Sure.'

I took his phone off the table and looked at it for a moment. It was in a black-book case and was much bigger than mine. In fact, it was very big. How beautiful Candy Crush must look on this! I thought to myself.

'I love your phone. Now, I've told you something about me, tell me about yourself.'

'I am sixteen years old; I turn seventeen in the fall. I'm in Sports High School. I have a driving license.'

'He is a master on the roads,' said Cătălin laughing.

'Wait, wait a minute. What do you mean you have a driving license? What kind of permit?' I asked, very surprised.

'Just a normal driver's license – anyone can once you are sixteen.'

'Really? How cool, I didn't know there was such a thing!'

'Yes, there is. Would you like something else to drink?' he asked, kindly.

'I, nothing, thank you. Juice and cappuccino are enough. I forgot to tell you that I like listening to music. So, I'm going to put on my headphones, and you can carry on your conversation, you needn't notice me.'

I took my headphones out of my bag, fastened them to my ears, and turned up the volume. I closed my eyes and had a think about what I would tell Magda. Alex looked like an ordinary guy, quite simple, nice, and unpretentious. Thinking about higher principles, if he is in the Sports High School, he probably doesn't like studying very much and he doesn't seem to have any big aspirations, and Magda is alike, so they found each other. The volume of the song dropped sharply. I had received a message.

Magda: Girl, say something!!

Me: What?

Magda: He is so handsome! I like him a lot!!

Me: And what should I do?

Magda: I don't know...

Magda was my best friend, she was the person I shared everything with, the person I trusted the most, I would have done anything for her...and I really did. Although she was two years older, we got along perfectly. Even though we were two completely opposite personalities, we somehow managed to agree on everything. We had known each other for about five years: we had been neighbours, and then after she moved, we continued to see each other.

Her parents divorced a long time ago. She was even separated from her younger sister, Georgiana. Magda stayed with her father, and Georgiana with her mother, but in fact she ended up staying with her grandparents from Botoșani, because her mother went to Italy, where she gave birth to another daughter, who also ended up in Botoșani. Magda was deprived of her mother's love and had no one to teach her what was good and what was wrong. Her father was not a good example either. He had been involved with two more women since I first met him. He was an unfriendly man. Somehow, I had been affected by her story and felt the need to be close to her. My parents had little contact with Magda's father.

They were not happy that I had such a good relationship with Magda, I often had arguments with them about it. When we were neighbours, and my mother cooked something nice, I would call Magda and we would eat together. My parents and I quarrelled about Magda countless times, after the last quarrel I promised myself never to talk to her again. But in the end, I did anyway. It seems that you cannot escape your destiny.

I took my headphones out to join the conversation. They were all laughing.

'Why are you laughing? Tell me, I want to laugh too!' I said smiling.

'Cătălin told me about how Alex drives, about how terrible he is!' Magda replied with a laugh.

'Well, not really. I said that sometimes he races through the city at a high speed, and I feel like we are in a rally, but otherwise he's okay. He's careful enough.'

'Is that so? Nice of you to praise your friend, Cătălin,' I replied.

'Not to boast, but I am really good!' said Alex, laughing.

'You make me curious,' I answered.

'Shall we take a tour through the town centre to show you? Come on.'

He got up from his chair first and took his keys out of his pocket, then I got up, taking my phone off the table.

'I'm leaving my bag here, Magda. Keep it safe till I get back,' I said laughing.

'Your bag's in good hands, don't worry.'

'The car's out the front. Shall we go?' Alex asked me.

'Sure.'

I followed Alex out of the cafe and got in the car. It was a small, grey, two-seater car. Before starting it, he connected some wires, which were down next to the gearbox. Then he turned on the tape recorder very loudly and started the car. The speakers blasted out with a very old, gypsy love song.

'Don't you have any modern music?'

'Yes, of course.'

'And ... how do you like Magda?'

'Magda? She's nice.'

'Really? And you are nice to her, really very nice?' I hinted.

And life is nice too. And it knows how to surprise you every time, especially when you least expect it. Especially when you feel like you are in control of everything and that nothing bad can happen to you. A second. It takes only a second to lose absolutely everything. It only takes a second for your entire perfect universe to turn into the worst nightmare. One second for everything you love to become everything you hate. One second for memories to become the only beautiful things in your life.

I didn't get to hear Alex's answer because as soon as we turned into Ana Ipătescu Street, he lost control of the steering wheel. We overturned and my side of the car smashed into a van. I didn't have time to realise we were going to have an accident. I didn't even see when he lost control of the steering wheel. It was a split second. It destroyed everything.

I saw Alex taking off his seat belt and getting out of the car. He had not been hurt. My lungs filled with the smell of fuel, oil, and everything else flowing from that car. I wanted to cry for help, but I couldn't make the sound. After several attempts, in a low and desperate voice I managed to shout. Time was running out and reality moving off. A lady who stopped as soon as she saw the accident climbed into the pile of metal where I was trapped, took me in her arms and pulled me onto the tarmac.

'How old are you?' asked a masculine voice.

'Thirteen.'

He was probably just a man who happened to be passing by. I couldn't see him. I could only see the pristine sky. I tried as hard as I could to breathe and stay awake.

'My phone. Please, bring me my phone.'

Several people had gathered around me. I couldn't see them, but I could hear them. Someone had brought me the phone, which kept ringing. It was probably Magda. The screen seemed fine, but the inside had been damaged. The display was filled with pixels, and whoever brought it to me couldn't turn it on.

'It's probably broken. None of the keys are working. Stay calm, the ambulance is on its way,' mumbled a woman.

The feelings I had in those moments cannot be described in words. I didn't know what was hurting me and where I had been hit, but I had a thousand sensations. Besides the pain and despair, I was terribly afraid of what was to come. I felt guilty. My parents believed I was in school. I felt guilty for agreeing to come with Magda instead of going to the headmistress's birthday. I felt guilty for agreeing to get in the car with a boy I didn't even know, and all that for the sake of my best friend. Even if I did not cause the accident, I was guilty. I could not stop thinking about my parents.

'Please … please don't let my parents know.' Those were the last words I said, consciously, on the tarmac. I did not pass out completely, but I think the afterlife was very close to me. I don't know how the paramedics put me on the stretcher and how they got me in the ambulance.

'Deep wound to the left upper limb', 'venous line', 'compress' were probably the words of the rescue nurses from the ambulance. They started to cut my clothes, and in the background, I could hear the equipment they had connected to me and the siren of the ambulance.

'Please don't cut my chain too!' I begged, then reality was swallowed again. I probably said more, but that's all I remember.

Part of me may have started travelling elsewhere. I don't know how they rescued me, how I got into the hospital, if I was in pain or not. I don't know what was happening to me.

I came back slightly when a lady asked me for my parents' address and phone numbers. I didn't hesitate and gave her my father's number. I knew that he was stronger and that he would not lose his temper when hearing the news that his only child was in hospital after a car accident. And that's how it was. The nurse or doctor who called my father did not give him much information about my condition, whether it was serious or not, but only told him to go to the Emergency Unit because I had been involved in an accident.

Dad had taken a bus to work that morning, so he didn't have his car. He managed to get permission from the bosses to leave and called his brother. My uncle was the second person to find out about my accident. He couldn't face calling my mother first.

'Good morning and happy birthday – excuse me if I'm bothering you ...' Dad said. (My uncle was born on March 27th and we had celebrated his birthday the day before with my family.)

'Hello, Sebica. Thank you very much. What are you doing? What's happened?'

'Someone called me from the emergency room and told me that Andreea had an accident, but they didn't want to tell me what happened, whether she was hurt or not ...'

'God forbid ... I'm coming to pick you up and let's go and see what's up.'

'I think maybe it's a joke. Or who knows? Maybe she was not looking and crossed the road carelessly. Come and get me, please. I'm waiting out on the street.'

'Sure, Sebica. I'm leaving now.'

Meanwhile my uncle informed my aunt, and she called my mum.

'Hi, Emma, can you talk?'

'Hello, Puşa, tell me quickly, I have to make the orders.'

'Emma ... Andreea has been in a car accident.'

'Which Andreea?'

Yes, this is how a person answers when they are not expecting life to deliver a blow. This was my mother's response, the answer of a woman who has not harmed anyone and expects life to answer her with the same currency.

'Emma ... Andreea, your Andreea, our Andreea.'

'Girl, are you crazy? Oh my God! And what's wrong with her? What happened? Is it serious?'

'I don't know. Sebica and Aronel are on their way to the hospital.'

'Oh my God! I've got to go too.'

'I'm coming with you. I'm leaving work now. See you at the station and we'll take a taxi, okay?'

'Okay.'

You never know how much life can surprise you until you are presented with the fait accompli. You never know if the words you say to your mother in the morning, in a hurry are, in fact, the last. You continue the routine you're used to, and you don't expect to be disturbed in any way, and when you are, you don't think it will be anything bad. You refuse to believe that the course of your life could change like this, suddenly, without being guilty of anything. You never get a warning that today may be the last day when you feel, love, joy, laughter. You are not ready to react when something serious happens. You are left with millions of unanswered questions that slowly kill you.

I could hear voices around me, but I couldn't concentrate on what they were saying. They did several investigations on me, and several doctors came to see me. I couldn't feel anything, and I couldn't move. I could see the ceiling, but it was all very foggy. I don't know if anyone told me anything. At some point my father appeared.

'Daddy, please forgive me, I promise to do anything you say,' I said almost crying.

'Stay calm, baby.' He replied with tears in his eyes.

'I can't feel anything anymore! Why?'

'You will feel ... calm down.'

'Am I going to die?'

'No, baby, no! You will not die.' Those were the last words I heard from my father at that time. 'The situation is serious. The MRI shows that she was hit in the spine, in the cervical area. She needs to get to the neurosurgery hospital urgently. We can't operate on her here. I will talk to my professor from the faculty, Dr Popescu, from the neurosurgery hospital in Iaşi, and we will transfer her there,' Dr Albu told my father.

My mother and aunt arrived at the hospital. I was wrapped in a white sheet, and when my mother saw me, she began to tremble. I didn't say much to her. All I know is that I told her to get closer to me because I couldn't see her. My uncle made a few calls to get me the best ambulance so that I could get to Iaşi as soon as possible. The whole family was trying to contribute in some way, through the influential people they had known over time. Magda appeared in the doorway. She had my blue bag in her hand. My mother couldn't stand her at the best of times, now she could hardly prevent herself from hitting her. Luckily, my aunt stopped her. My mother never liked Magda. Not even when we were younger. She always told me that I had nothing to learn from her and that she was a negative influence on me.

'What are you doing here? Why is her bag with you? I told you to leave Andreea alone? Go away!' my mother shouted at Magda.

'I don't know what happened, I don't know anything, I am so sorry! What happened? Is it serious?' Magda replied, trembling.

'What do you mean you don't know? You are a liar! Aren't you ashamed? Get out of here, I don't want to see you!' cried my mother.

You never know how close a friend is to you until you're on the edge of the abyss. You never know if the person you share all your secrets with would jump into the fire to save you or would leave you there to burn. You never know if the individual who you gave the title 'best friend' is truly worthy of the name. When I say friend, I think of the highest qualities. I think, first, of respect. Then I think of love, generosity, devotion, trust, wisdom, responsibility. I think of the whole beauty of creation God made in each human. A true friend is one who, regardless of the situation, is close to you. A true friend is one who stays by your side even if you have lost a leg, a hand. Even if you have lost your skills. A true friend is someone who does not judge but advises. A true friend is one who, if you have lost your sight, makes your soul see all that the eyes cannot. They are a pillar that never falls, there regardless of the disasters in life. A friend is the one who lifts you up when life is hard and shows you how close the sun is to you. The others are just acquaintances. But how many of us have even one friend? How many of us succeed in being a friend? How many of us respect and love the one next to us?

Meanwhile, a surgeon came and looked at my left hand. Almost all the formalities were complete, and we were preparing to leave. There was a great commotion.

'What did you not understand? I said I want adrenaline! A whole box!,' a doctor shouted desperately at the nurse who had come with only two ampoules, probably not knowing how serious my condition was.

One of the nurses there was related to Angela, my aunt's sister-in-law, so she came to my aunt and holding her hand said, 'It's very serious... if she makes it, the child will never walk again.' My aunt didn't want to believe those words.

Ramona, my cousin, came to the hospital with Miruna, her daughter. I had already been moved to the ambulance. My eyes were closed as Ramo got into the ambulance to talk to me. She grabbed my hand, but I didn't respond.'

'Kiss her on the forehead,' the doctor whispered to Ramona.

When I felt the kiss on my forehead, I opened my eyes. My face was the only area where I could feel anything.

'Ramo,' I said almost crying, 'What is happening to me? I can't feel anything!'

'You will be fine! Be strong, we are by your side!'

Everything was ready, so the ambulance started its siren and we set off. We embarked on a road with few options and no way out; on a road I could not have imagined even in my worst nightmares. I was accompanied by a doctor and a nurse. The main goal was not to fall asleep. The medical crew did everything they could to keep me awake. It was hard for me to keep my eyes open. I kept closing them, and when I opened them, I could see my reflection in the roof of the ambulance. I saw a helpless person. A person wrapped in a white sheet, who was connected to a machine that made noises, noises that still signalled signs of life. It seemed like an eternity passed since the ambulance collected me and from time to time, I asked how long it would take to get there. I was answered gently each time. Everything seemed like a distant present, as if time had stopped and I was outside of it. Behind the ambulance were my parents, accompanied by my aunt and uncle. I can't imagine the feelings they were experiencing when the flashing lights started and, in those moments, I'm sure they felt like they didn't have enough air in their lungs, and that their hearts were in their throats.

An hour and a bit had passed before we arrived at the neurosurgery hospital in Iași. All the medical staff into whose hands my life was placed were waiting in front of the hospital. Sami, Ramona's husband, happened to be there with a friend who had come for a check-up. The doctor opened the ambulance door and they got ready to take me out.

'Please help! Someone take the monitor. Quick!' cried the doctor desperately.

'Ma'am, I'm the girl's aunt. Please tell me what to do!' replied my aunt to the doctor's shout from the ambulance.

'Pray!' was the doctor's answer. My aunt remained silent. It was too much of an answer. An answer she didn't even know how to interpret. Pray for my recovery or just my survival, no matter the circumstances? An answer from which you no longer know what to expect or whether to have any more expectations. An answer with which you entrust your life to the hands of God, and you only hope that everything will end well.

They took me straight to the ICU ward; my condition was getting worse. Every possible sensation and pain were hitting me, I started screaming in despair and fear. They did tests and prepared me. My parents were in the doctor's office. They were told that there was going to be an operation. They were presented with the whole situation and signed the pre-operation consent.

At 2 p.m., the light in the operating room came on. The doctors were working for my survival, struggling for my existence, because that was all they could do. They removed the splinters from the spinal cord, splinters belonging to the vertebra that shattered in the accident. Then they rebuilt the vertebra, taking a bone graft from my hip and securing it with screws and plates.

The operation was a success, but it could not give me my previous life back.

After three and a half hours they took me to a recovery room. My parents and relatives were waiting for news from the doctors. They were near the elevator when they saw Dr Popescu taking off his cap with one hand, while with his other hand he wiped his forehead, sighing loudly. It was not a sigh of tiredness or the hard work of operating, but a sigh for my life, for what remained of it after that operation. He knew the consequences of such trauma. He knew the pain that would follow in my life. When they saw this, my parents went up to him.

'Doctor how is she?' my father asked.

'Pray! She survived, but we can't know what will happen next. The first few hours are critical. Let's first wait twenty-four, forty-eight, seventy-two hours and then see how her condition evolves. If she leaves the hospital in a wheelchair, it'll be a miracle!'

In the face of such situations, you don't even know how to react and how to behave. You don't understand how a day that had started like any other could turn into a nightmare. You look for the culprits, you ask yourself thousands of questions and you cling to hope. You are angry, so angry and do not know who to blame for what is happening to you. Who can you fight with and strangle for causing all the suffering? You do not understand why God has given you so many things, only to take them away, in an instant, without having done anything wrong. Without a cause. You wonder what you did wrong, that means your only child has lost all her dreams. Millions of 'whys' remain unanswered, and you are crushed by every moment.

They took me to a room, to a bed near the wall. There was another girl in the room, she was also called Andreea. She was in a coma after a car accident. I have no memory of the first moments after the operation. Someone wiped my mascara and tied my hair up with a bandage. Later in the evening, my parents, my uncle and my aunt were given permission to come in to see me. I couldn't tell them what had happened. I started screaming. I was suffocating. The doctors came quickly and intubated me. After all this, my family had to return to Bacău. So, constrained by the situation and with a heavy heart, they went home. I don't know what was in my parents' souls when they entered the house, knowing that I was on a hospital bed with few chances of survival. They probably cried until the morning, when they packed some clothes and my teddy bear, and returned to Iași. In a different place, at three in the morning, my uncle and my aunt, coming from different bedrooms, met on the landing, where they looked into each other's eyes and burst into tears.

In the morning, all my acquaintances had found out about my accident and mobilised as best they could to raise money. We were a modest family. We couldn't afford too much. We didn't go on vacation, as other people do. We went to Durau, in the mountains once. My family made sacrifices so that I would not feel the lack of money. They wanted to give me everything I needed. And they managed to do it. I saw the sea for the first time thanks to them. They raised money so that I could go to Eforie by the sea, last year, with the dance ensemble. The same happened with the trip to Istanbul. They didn't buy anything for themselves so that I could have everything I needed. Every month, half of the money from their salaries went to bills and the mortgage of the flat. There was no month where they did not borrow money from relatives, or pawn gold so that we could manage to the next salary date. Maybe it was hard, but I didn't feel it, because we were happy. We were healthy together, and that was all that mattered.

In those days, relatives, acquaintances, strangers, neighbours, co-workers of my mother and father, friends and relatives, all mobilised and raised money for me. They all went hand in hand together for life. For my life. People to whom I give thanks with all my heart and wish them all the best in the world.

2

How do I breathe?

It is more than thirty-five hours since the accident. Friday night edging into early Saturday morning. I am aware of what is happening to me and around me. In the hospital room, the light is still on. Probably because of me. I can't see much. I can't move at all. I hear the device monitoring my vital functions. I can barely breathe, even though I am wearing an oxygen mask. I feel like vomiting and coughing. I hear footsteps. Someone is approaching my bed. A nurse. There are secretions in my throat that I can't get rid of. He puts some suction catheters down my nose, then down my throat to suck them up. I start to get agitated because the tubes are very uncomfortable.

'I know it's not nice, but you have to put up with me and let me do the suction,' said the nurse.

'I can't breathe, and I feel like throwing up,' I replied.

'When I have finished you will be able to breathe more easily.' I opened my mouth and let him do what he had to do. It was a terrible, horrible feeling. I felt out of breath. In those moments I kept asking myself what made me deserve this torture? Why was I going through with it?

'I've finished. I'll put the oxygen mask back on. Is that better?'

'No. I'm so sorry.'

'What bothers you the most?'

'Everything. I don't know what hurts the most, but I can't cope anymore. Can you make me fall asleep?'

'You had a sedative an hour ago. You have to finish the other bottles in the infuser before you have another.'

'What about a sleeping pill?'

'We can't give that to you. Try to calm down. I have to check the other patients as well.'

'Can't you stay with me a bit longer? I don't want to be alone.'

'I will ask another nurse to come.'

'Ok.'

'What's your name?'

'Andreea,' I answered. He looked at me strangely, then left.

I couldn't fall asleep. I tried to look around, but I couldn't see much. I couldn't move my head either. I don't know what caused the most suffering: the physical pain, the despair that I couldn't move or make any gestures, or the fear that I couldn't breathe properly even with the oxygen mask on.

All these states were amplifying every second, and the desperate attempts the rational part of me made to convince myself that tomorrow would be better were overshadowed by the excruciating pain in my soul. Finally, it was morning. There was a great commotion in the corridor. One nurse administered treatment to me intravenously, and two others came to wash me. They were warned not to move me too much, to let me stay on my back so as not to increase the chance of complications from the operation.

'How are you feeling Alexandra?' one of the nurses asked me.

'Not good. My head is hurting as well. Why do you call me Alexandra?'

'Isn't that your name? That's what it says on your chart.'

'It's my middle name. Nobody ever calls me that. Everybody calls me Andreea.'

'Alexandra is a very beautiful name too. I'm going to get a thermometer and a Perfalgan. Looks like you have a fever.'

Now I understood why the nurse last night had looked at me strangely when I told him my name was Andreea. He must have thought that I had forgotten my name. I thought about this with a hint of amusement.

'Let's check your temperature. How long has your head been hurting for?'

'I don't know. Could someone put a clock on the wall? – then at least I could stare at something other than the ceiling.'

'We'll see about that. Yes, you have a fever, 38.7ºc. I'm giving you Perfalgan and I hope it helps your headache to go away. How is your breathing?'

'The same... Why can't I move yet? What operation did I have?'

'You have to be patient, be very patient. I am going to check on two other patients and then I will come back to aspirate you.'

'Again? But I don't like it, I don't want it anymore. Please!'

'You have to, Alexandra. It is a must. I'll be right back.'

As the nurse headed for the door, another nurse came in.

'Good morning, Alexandra, how are you? I understand you don't like being alone. I'm here to stay with you a while,' she said with a smile.

'Good morning. Thank you for coming. What's your name?'

'Violeta. How was last night? I heard you didn't feel well and couldn't sleep.'

'Yeah – I've had better days. I can't breathe, I feel so tired, but I still can't fall asleep.'

'You are strong, Alexandra. You will get better, you will see.'

'When?'

'Soon. Don't give up.'

'Alexandra, Alexandra, you have a lot of visitors waiting to see you,' said a new nurse as she bustled into the room.

'So why haven't they come in?'

'They are not allowed just now. They are waiting in the corridor. They will come in to see you at visiting time.'

'Why?'

'This ward is for seriously ill patients; you all need to be protected from infections.'

'Am I seriously ill too?'

'Alexandra ... you had an accident and suffered severe trauma. Your body needs to be protected.'

'Where was I hit? I can't move and I can't feel my body. If you put your hands on me, I can't feel you. I can't feel the butterfly needle. I can't even feel the blanket on me. I feel nothing! Why?'

'We don't know yet, Alexandra. You must be patient. We're going to turn some patients and will come back to you later, okay?'

'Okay, but what do you mean by "turn" them?'

Turn them onto their side with the sheet. They can't move. They are like you. In a few days, after the doctor assures us that we will not aggravate the operation site, we will turn you too, every four hours, so that you don't get bed sores. Until then, the mattress will protect you.

'I understand. Go to them.'

In the meantime, a different nurse came, aspirated me and took blood for some tests. My despair at not being able to move kept growing.

It was one p.m., visitor's hour. Mum, Dad, Uncle, Aunt and Magda came. They were not allowed to all enter at once, so they came in in pairs. Mum and Dad had brought me my favourite teddy bear, which slept by my pillow at home every night.

'Nurse, can Andreea, eat chocolate?' my aunt asked.

'Yes, but only white.'

'Sure, thank you.' My aunt went down to the store in front of the hospital and bought me white chocolate with whole hazelnuts while I talked to Magda.

'How do you feel?' Magda asked me.

'Not too well. I can't move at all! I think you and Diana will have to go to the prom without me. Dress nicely!'

'Andreea, you have to get well! I will try to visit as often as I can. How can we talk?'

'I don't know – in the evening I think there is another visiting hour – I'll tell my mother to call you and put my phone on the pillow so we can talk.

'That's what we'll do! Get well soon, we need you!'

'I'll try, but it's not up to me...'

'I'll let your parents in now. I love you so much!'

My aunt returned with the chocolate. She entered the room with my parents and uncle.

'Honey, I'll break it into small pieces, and you can it chew slowly, right? Be careful not to choke.'

'Yes.'

I was learning to eat and drink water while lying down – though this was probably the easiest thing I had to learn anew after what had happened to me.

'Is it good?' my mother asked me.

'Very good, can I have some water?' I replied.

'Aunty also brought you orange juice. Do you want some?'

'Yes.'

'Do you want it from a cup so you can drink with the straw, or should I give it to you with the syringe? What's easier for you?'

'Put it in the cup. Fill it right up and lift the straw as high as you can so that it reaches my mouth.'

'I told you to come in one at a time, maximum two people at once!' exclaimed a nurse who had just entered the room.

Dad and Uncle left the room while Mum and Aunt stayed. I really wanted to know more about what was happening to me. I was so desperate that I started to shake.

'Aunty, why can't I move? I've had surgery for appendicitis before and it wasn't like this. Why am I still numb? Why? Mum, what's going on?' I said almost crying.

'Andreuța, darling, calm down,' my mother replied with tears in her eyes.

'You'll be fine, baby.' soothed my aunt.

'But I can't stand it anymore, I want to get out of here!'

'I know, Andreea, but we have to be patient... don't cry, okay? It will be fine!'

'Okay, but I can't wait too long. I feel something tight around my chin. What is it?'

'It is the edge of the collar that holds your neck.'

'Why do I need a collar?'

'Andreea ... you had surgery on your spine, in the cervical area. The collar keeps your neck steady so that no complications occur.'

'It feels horrible. It's made of a very rigid material.'

'We will talk to the doctor or a nurse, perhaps they can change it.'

'Visiting time is almost over. The men can come in quickly for five minutes, and then you must all leave, said the nurse.'

'Nurse, could you change her collar, please? It's irritating her chin.'

'I think that's possible, but you'll have to buy a different one. You'd better talk to Dr Popescu, he's on duty.'

'Thank you! Baby, be strong. Daddy and I are going to talk to the doctor and wait in the corridor until the next visiting hour. See you tonight,' said my mother, smiling with tears in her eyes.

'Your uncle and I are taking Magda back home now. I promise we'll come in the next few days,' said my aunt. 'I think Ramona will come tomorrow.'

'Okay, I love you. Let Daddy and Uncle come in now.'

'We love you too! So very much!' my mother said, kissing me on the forehead.

My dad and uncle reappeared at the door.

'Daddy, talk to the doctor, please, to change my collar.'

'Sure will! See you tonight. Be strong. Mother and I will be in the corridor.'

'Kisses to you, darling! You are the bravest!' added Uncle.

They all left, and I was alone with my anxiety and the noise of the medical equipment in the room. In less than five minutes three nurses came to me.

'I hope you haven't come to do any more torture procedures!' I told them when I saw that there were so many.

'No, Alexandra, no. We came to sit together to swap stories,' said one of them, amused.

'What did you like to do at home, Alexandra? How can we cheer you up?' asked another nurse.

I think they stayed with me for over an hour. They told me about themselves and their families. They even gave me a manicure with turquoise nail polish – but only on two fingers – because a nurse said that if all the nails were painted with nail polish, they wouldn't be able to monitor my oxygen saturation. But I was content with two nails, and it was great to have company. They even made me laugh telling me how upset they were about what was written in the new labour protection protocol. In the corridor my parents talked to the doctor. He approved a less rigid collar and told them to look for ACC aerosols in the hope that they would improve my breathing. My parents went to orthopaedic shops and to the pharmacy to buy all the things.

'I want more water, please.'

'Alexandra, you have drunk a lot already. Are you feeling alright? Should we call a senior nurse?'

'I don't know, but I'm always thirsty,' I replied. I could feel my throat drying out, and my face was burning, I could hardly tell what reality was.

'Alexandra, how do you feel? Can you hear me?' a nurse asked me.

'I feel like I'm suffocating, do something, please!'

'Don't panic, stay calm. The oxygen is on maximum. Focus on breathing. I'll bring a sedative and treatment.'

It was a very hard day, followed by a night on the edge. I did not understand why I had to experience these limits. Me, less than fourteen years old. I did not understand why I had to suffer and face so much evil. I just wanted to fall asleep, so that at least for a few hours I would not feel all the pain and sensations that were bothering me. I wanted to fall asleep, not to face my difficulty breathing through those long hours, not to feel like I was suffocating. To feel nothing. I didn't want to live.

After the morning rounds, the doctors took me to the operating room, to try to do something for my left hand, a hand that I didn't know was injured, believing that everything I was going through was more than enough for one child. I could see the huge bright lights of the operating theatre. The radio was playing "One Day," sung by Arash. When I heard the song, I told myself that one day I would see the sunlight and feel the moon on my face again. I can't picture how my left hand was damaged in that car but almost all the flesh on the palm was torn, my ring finger was also broken in three and the skin torn off. My mother begged the doctors not to amputate it, which was their original plan. So instead, the surgeon tried to reconstruct my crushed finger and remove the residue from the little skin that remained, then he fixed my hand and forearm with plaster.

Two more terrible days passed in the same style: fever, shortness of breath, not even a minute of sleep, agony and constant anxiety. The hours spent with my parents were the happiest, otherwise time passed terribly slowly. On Monday, around noon, they moved me to a new room to protect me from infections, then a doctor and a nurse came to change the bandage on my left hand.

'I want to see my hand, please.' I told them.

'Are you sure?' the doctor asked me.

'Very.'

I can't say that I've seen a lot of horror movies, but I've seen a few and I haven't seen anything that looks uglier than my hand. The wrist to the fingers was a skeleton on which stood a few patches that tried to resemble skin. The ring finger, also skinless, no longer looked like a finger, but was a small, deformed bone at the end of which was the nail. I wonder how the whole nail stayed on.

'I have seen enough, thank you. When will it be normal?'

'In about eight weeks' – meaning never. It was just an answer thrown at me to stop me bothering them any further – and it was beneficial for me at that moment – because I really thought that my hand would heal and look like before. I thought that all the situations in this world had a solution that would bring them back to their original form. A solution that gave a second chance. But, along the way, I found out I was wrong. I have learned that most choices and actions in this world are irreversible and that no one and nothing can offer a second chance. I learned that in most cases, once you lose something, you lose it forever.

3

Life on a thread

Another ten days went by that were just as bad. Two weeks had passed since the accident that turned my life upside down. Two weeks of torment, agony, horror and pain. Two weeks in which my life hung by a thread. Days when the next second didn't seem certain. Days when even the doctors didn't know what to do – they were waiting for a miracle. There were several times my parents were told to prepare for the worst – there was even a suggestion that they should buy me a coffin.

In those two weeks my parents and the nurses did everything they could to get a smile out of me. One day, a nurse put make-up on me. Another day, two nurses washed my hair with a special cape used for people who are bedridden. Then a nurse braided my hair. Thanks to the director of the hospital, my parents could visit me outside of visiting hours. Because it was an intensive care unit, there were no televisions in the wards. My parents were allowed to bring me one, but there was no cable and the TV only had one channel. They also brought me a radio. They did everything they could to try to bring me a drop of joy.

I was moved every three to four days to a different hospital room, freshly disinfected, to protect me from bacteria. Now, I am in a room at the front. There are only two beds. I can see the entrance of the hospital perfectly. New people and new stories enter every day. But every day, the same entrance lets out at least one person with a white sheet covering their head. A nurse walks on either side of the trolley. I imagine the person who has departed – most likely, sad and lonely, because there was no time to say goodbye to loved ones. Also beyond that door are my parents, waiting to come in and see me. From this room, I can hear the noises of the devices that monitor the other patients. I can also hear the long beep which means that the ECG line has gone flat forever.

My ECG line almost went flat. There were days when I could barely breathe. They tried all possible options to give me an extra mouthful of oxygen. My parents searched all the pharmacies in search of ACC for aerosols, and finally found some. There were days when I had high fevers and unbearable pain. Other days there were new sensations I was forced to get used to. I felt like my knees were burning as if someone had put me in an oven. Muscle spasms arrived in my lower limbs, involuntary movements in my legs, which appeared and disappeared as and when they wanted. The leg simply rose, and then fell, or the whole limb trembled. Although I was uncomfortable, I enjoyed the spasms, believing that they were part of the healing process. Now, I know that the spasms are extremely aggressive and harmful. I would like them to disappear forever, but that is not possible. My whole body had been turned upside down. I had started drinking a lot of water. One day, I drank twelve litres.

I spent most nights with the nurses. I could not close my eyes. I made friends with all the medical staff on the ICU department, impeccable staff, in all regards. On a few evenings, when I had slightly more energy, my mother would hold the phone to my ear so that I could talk to Magda and all those who, at the time, were dear to me and seemed close to me. Other evenings, I could barely utter a few words. It was terribly hard for me to see my parents leave helpless and upset that they couldn't do more for me.

My mother was always more sensitive and emotional. It was normal to see her with tears on her cheeks, although she tried to hold them back as much as she could, especially in front of me. In contrast, my father is, and has always been an extremely strong, upright and balanced man. A man I have only seen cry once or twice in my near fourteen years of life. One evening, while I was talking to the two of them, my father looked at me and burst into tears. That was the first time that I realised how precarious my situation was.

4

Will I be able to walk?

It was a little after five-thirty p.m. A new shift had just started, including Mrs Lili, a nurse I was attached to. She had come to talk to me, and I asked her to feed me cherry compote.

'That's a good sign, Alexandra. I'm glad you're eating.'

'Well, there should be good signs. Maybe I'll get better and go home.'

'You have to stay a while longer, Alexandra.'

I was irritated. 'I'd like to go out. Feel the fresh air. See the sun, the clouds and the people roaring in the streets. Can't you take me out of bed or put me on a stretcher in front of the hospital, please?'

'And what would we do with the devices that monitor you?'

'We could give them a break.'

'Even the oxygen?'

'Yes. The fresh air will help me.'

'It's not possible Alexandra. I'm sorry.'

'Pfft ... Have there been other cases like this around here?'

'There have been, Alexandra... there have been.'

'How long did they stay in the hospital and when did they start walking?'

'Well, they didn't really start to walk. There was another boy, just like you, with a similar spine injury. I'm still in touch with him. He has been in many hospitals; he recovered his hands but is in a wheelchair.'

'I'll be much better than him. I'll walk, you'll see.'

'So be it, Alexandra.'

I appreciated Mrs Lili's sincerity, but I didn't want to believe her words. I couldn't believe that someone could be so permanently damaged at such a young age because of a car accident. I probably couldn't believe it because I had no knowledge of spinal cord injuries and because I didn't know they could cause full paralysis. The fact that I did not give credibility to what I heard gave me the strength to carry on, to wait for a reality that I wanted.

Some good signs had appeared which helped me believe I could recover. I regained mobility and sensitivity in my neck after the doctor removed the wires from the operation and took off the front of my collar. Now I could turn my head from side to side. The nurses had also started to turn my body from side to side, but not every four hours, only when I allowed them to. I did not like the manoeuvres or being on my side. I had no control over my body, so it was terribly scary when someone moved me. The electric bed allowed the nurses to raise my torso to about thirty-five degrees. The first time they did it I felt like I was out of breath and my eyesight darkened, then I got used to it. I liked that I could see what was around me.

Silviu, the physiotherapist, had also started gently mobilising my limbs to avoid muscle and tendon retraction as much as possible. Sometimes he would tap me to help me remove the secretions from my throat, which usually I only got rid of if I was suctioned. Things seemed to settle down, but this was just an impression. It was nothing lasting.

'Alexandra, I have good news and I have less good news,' Mrs Lili told me.

'Hmm, what's the good news?'

'At night you will be able to sleep. We'll give you something to help you.'

'Amazing! I can't wait. What about the less good news?

'The butterfly needle is clogged.'

'I don't like it, but I accept the situation. It was probably happy for me when it heard I was going to sleep at night,' I replied with a chuckle.

'Great. I'm going to bring new butterflies,' replied Mrs Lili, laughing.

I had become accustomed to the states and pains. I had even got used to my difficult breathing. I tried to face the daily challenges and I really succeeded. Even the doctor who operated on me had started joking with me. Although the diagnosis was not encouraging, I was trying to defy it. All this in the hope that tomorrow would be better for me.

5

Helpless in the face of fate

Today, I had lots of visitors. My parents, my aunt, uncle, cousin and grandmother. I was very happy to be surrounded by people dear to my heart.

'Andruşca, my love, how are you, darling?'

'Hello Granny a little better, I think, but I still can't really move. I can feel and turn my neck though.'

'My love, you are young and you will recover, you will see.'

'Yeah… I hope it happens soon. I'm going crazy. I can't stand this situation anymore.'

'No, my dear, don't talk like that! You are a strong one, you always have been. We are always here with you to support you.'

Grandmother, my father's mother, had always been dear to me. A very good woman, loving and generous. I remember the summer holidays I spent with her and my father in the country with great fondness. Grandfather was an extremely handsome man, with serene and tender blue eyes and an exemplary character. He died far too early. I was there when it happened in 2008, at the beginning of January. I was a little over seven years old. He had been hospitalised immediately after New Year's Eve, and on January 8th he was discharged. He had problems with his heart and pancreas. My father collected him from the hospital, then they came to fetch me from school. We went to their village. He seemed fine. Nothing foretold that in the next few hours he would only exist in our memories.

When we arrived in the country, Grandmother was waiting for us with food on the table. Grandad didn't eat much, just some soup. We were all talking when, suddenly, he put on his shoes and went outside without saying anything. He probably felt like his end was coming and he didn't want me to see. We thought he needed to go to the toilet. After a few minutes, grandmother went out.

'Sebica, Sebica! Come quickly, Mitica is dying!'

Although I was quite small and was not expecting to witness death, I shuddered when I heard my grandmother's cries. Dad went out quickly, and I stayed in the house.

'Go call for the ambulance and call Nicu,' father told my grandmother.

Granddad was lying on the floor, still breathing. There were only the two of them, father and son. My father tried to give him a heart massage and mouth-to-mouth breathing, but without success. Meanwhile, Nicu, the neighbour, had come.

'What's going on, Sebi?'

'Nicu, bring a candle'

'Sebi, no ...'

'Go, Nicu, go!'

It's terrible for your father to die in your arms. The father who held you in his arms until yesterday. They brought him into the house in a blanket, where he gave his last breath. I see him even now, lying on the floor, in the middle of the room, without any power and with a candle at his head. Grandad, a man of the mountains, who made me swings in the tree every summer that fulfilled all my desires, was now beside me, but he could no longer do anything for us, and we couldn't do anything for him. Sooner or later that's how we all end up. Helpless in the face of fate. And we remain just a memory. A memory we have to take care of throughout our lives.

'I brought you yogurt with burnt sugar. Do you want some?' my aunt asked me. 'How are you, my little one?'

'I don't know, aunty, but I'm bored here. I think I'm going to run away.'

'Andreea, if you do that, I promise no one will be upset,' Aunty answered, thinking of the prognosis given by the doctors.

6

Dead sleep

It was evening, and I was looking forward to the medicine that would help me sleep – I could not keep going any longer.

A nurse bustled up to me, 'Alexandra, Alexandra, you have a fever again! Why are you bothering me again?' she joked.

'I don't think I can handle it anymore...'

'You must, at least for your parents.'

'I'm almost at the end of my powers ... your colleague said this morning that you would give me something to help me sleep.'

'Yes, but I can't give that to you until the fever has gone down. I gave you Perfalgan and if your temperature goes down in an hour, I will also give you diazepam so you can get some sleep.

Luckily for me, my fever dropped after an hour, and the nurse came with the diazepam syringe. She gave me an intramuscular injection in my thigh. As soon as she finished injecting, I saw her getting up from her chair. I fell asleep instantly, unable to say anything. Only sleep did not seem the right word – only sensation, without dreams, without anything. When I woke up, I was even more tired, but at least a few hours of torment had passed that I did not have to bear consciously.

After the doctors' rounds in the morning, my parents came to me. They brought me milk with cocoa and mini croissants with vanilla and cherries.

'Were you able to sleep last night, baby?' my mother asked me.

'It didn't feel like sleep, so I can't say I slept. It all went black as soon as she gave me the injection, then I woke up around four, suddenly. Like someone forced me. I didn't even have dreams ...'

'Maybe tonight it will be better,' said my mother, kissing my hand.

'I hope ... By the way, one more died.'

'How do you know, honey? Who told you?'

'No one, but I saw them taking him out the door. He was wrapped in a white sheet.'

'No one died, darling. Most likely they took him to have an ultrasound.'

'Right? And they wrapped the sheet around his head so that the draught wouldn't affect him from the hall? I can't move, but my eyes are still good.'

'I don't know, dear, He was probably going for an MRI.'

'Yeah, that's right, as you say. Whose phone is ringing...'

'It's yours. It's an unknown number. Do you want to talk?'

'Yes. Answer and hold it to my ear please.'

'Sure.'

'Hello?'

'How are you Andreea?' It was a male voice, that I didn't recognise.

'Not very well, who is it?'

'Alex ... from the accident.' It seemed strange to me that he was calling after more than two weeks. 'How do you feel?'

'I can't feel anything from my neck down and I can't move at all, so not very well.'

'I understand. I hope you feel better. Speedy recovery.'

'Thank you.'

The phone rang off.

'Who was it?' my curious mother asked me.

'Alex, from the accident.'

'Why did you talk to him? Don't you hate him?

'No, why should I hate him? He didn't mean that to happen,' I replied to my mother very firmly.

But had I known that I was going to live through six more years of hell without a face-to-face conversation with him, without an apology or any recognition of how he had changed my life, I think my answer would have been different. He should have apologised, or said something about what happened, something. I'm not saying I hate him, I don't know how to hate people, but I don't like him either. I can't ignore his attitude to me.

7

Another hospital

Two hard days passed, and my parents were called to Dr Popescu's office.

'We should consider the option of a transfer. Alexandra is more stable and can withstand the journey. How about your local hospital in Bacau?

'Certainly not. Please, Doctor, anywhere else!' my father replied.

'Then we will try at Nicolina Hospital, here, in Iaşi. It's a recovery hospital. We need to take this step. We could keep her here but really Alexandra needs a different environment. In the morning, during my visit, she counted all the patients who have died since she has been here. It does her no good. She is quite affected by it. She lives and she will survive. The psychologist sees her every day, but she needs time. We need her to move on to the next stage of her recovery, we cannot afford to lose her mentally. I hope you understand.'

'Of course, we understand, thank you for the help.'

'Good. Then we will prepare her for the transfer to Nicolina.'

When I heard that they were going to take me to another hospital, I was somehow saddened. I had gotten used to the people here, especially Mrs Lili. But I was also happy, thinking that being in a recovery hospital would help my healing. They completed all the transfer documents and in two days we were off to the new hospital. On transfer day I was dressed for the first time since the accident. My parents bought me some new clothes. They had to be light, with buttons, so that I wouldn't be handled too much when they dressed me.

In the morning, the nurses washed and dressed me, then we waited for the ambulance so we could leave. They put on my cervical collar, lay me on a stretcher and we set off. After almost three weeks, I finally saw the light of day directly. Initially, I couldn't keep my eyes open. I blinked a few times and succeeded. It started to rain, and a splash of water settled on my face. That's when I realised how privileged we humans are to be able to see the sky and to have the fresh air invade our nostrils.

After about twenty minutes we arrived at the new hospital, where I was met by a nice doctor.

'Will I get better?' I asked her.

'Looking at your beautiful eyes, I would say yes,' she answered me. It was an encouraging answer, an answer that matched the reality I wanted and was looking forward to.

They took me to a room where there were two other older women and put me in the bed they had prepared. I was happy because my parents were allowed to stay with me. However, on inspecting the room, I realised that it was not what I expected.

'Mom, the windows don't have handles, and I really need air! You told me I would be taken to a recovery hospital, not a psychiatric hospital.'

'I will talk to a nurse and ask if they can open at least one window.'

'Please, go now and tell them. My head doesn't fit either. This mattress is different from the one I had at the other hospital.'

'I'm going after the doctor.' My father left the ward.

It was a desolate landscape. A very old room, without facilities. Although a recovery hospital, the bed didn't even have a pressure-sore mattress. The windows without handles made me anxious. I felt like I was in a sanatorium for the mentally ill. The old women were not very communicative. There was no TV, and a great silence filled the air. I wondered what I was doing here.

'Tell me, my dear, how can I help you?' asked the doctor.

'I need an open window and a different kind of mattress. My head feels as though it is on a boulder.'

'We don't have other mattresses – no anti-pressure sore mattresses. If you need one, your parents will have to buy it.'

'Sure. Just tell me where,' my father replied.

'I will write the name of the shop for you on a piece of paper.'

'And the window?' I asked again.

'I'm afraid we can't do anything about that.'

This is what Romania looked like in 2014. And this was just the beginning. A recovery hospital that does not even meet the minimum standards of a hospital. It is outrageous and inhuman not to have anti-pressure sore mattresses to prevent bed sores on the patients. It is a form of death sentence, as bedsores can lead to septicaemia, which often ends with the death of the person. I understand that when patients have a high mobility and can turn around on their own, the lack of an anti-pressure sore mattress might be accepted, but when the patient is completely immobilised (as is my case), what happens to them? What if the family doesn't have the money to buy the mattress? The hospital should offer them one, but it doesn't. What happens is that those responsible shrug their shoulders and pass the blame from one to the other, without anyone taking action, and people suffering have to endure it.

There are other ugly situations that people have to deal with in the hospital, such as no triage system or induction of patients. The diagnosis and age are not taken into consideration, and there is no one to talk to you about what is happening to your body. But, even worse, not having a source of clean air in a ward, given that we are talking about a recovery hospital and a ward where there are depressed and mentally ill people, is terrible. It is even more terrible to be a thirteen-year-old child going through all this.

My mother started unpacking, while my father went to an orthopaedic store to buy the mattress. I wasn't feeling well, and I needed to drink a lot of water again. My temperature felt like it was going crazy.

'Mom, I'm sick! Call someone, please!'

'What is happening, baby? Don't panic.'

'I can't breathe again, I need air. I think I also have a fever.'

'I'm going to the duty room.'

'How are you, sweetheart?' the doctor, who came with a nurse, asked me.

'I'm not feeling too well. I need air.'

'Yes, you are hot – you sure have a fever! Do you want to take a paracetamol?'

'At the other hospital, they always put it into my veins. I don't think I can take pills lying in bed. Can't you put something into my veins?'

'Okay. A nurse will come and do something for you. Make sure you are drinking water.'

I've already drunk too much. About five litres already.

'Oh, not like that! Try to reduce the amount as much as you can. Your whole body is turned upside down and you have to help it by controlling yourself.'

'I'm trying.'

In the meantime, the nurse with the intravenous fluid drip came and – guess what – the butterfly needle clogged, again. Initially, the nurse tried to fit the needle in my right hand, because the left one had plaster up to the elbow, and when she couldn't succeed, she tried my feet, which were very swollen and bruised from the butterflies of the past days. She couldn't manage and tried my right hand again, where she finally found a good vein. She gave me a sedative and something for the fever. By then, Dad had arrived with the mattress and some good food.

'Andreea, don't you want to eat something?' my father asked me.

'I don't feel able to and I don't feel like it. You had better put my new mattress on the bed.'

'Okay. I'm going to find a nurse or two to help us.' What nurse could help us, when this was the first time they had seen a case like mine?

The nurses brought a stretcher, and my parents explained to them what to do, based on what they had learnt at the ICU. They tried to move me together, transferring me with a sheet onto a stretcher before taking care of the mattress. It took them around thirty minutes to do this, and then they transferred me back to the bed.

'Is that better?'

'It's better. Thank you from the bottom of my heart, Daddy.'

'No problem. Come on, can't you eat something?

'No. You and mum should eat.'

It was getting harder and harder for me to bear everything that was happening to me. I didn't know what else to say in my mind to encourage myself. I no longer knew how to control myself – how to not break down and to stay rational. I felt somehow guilty, so I was pushing myself beyond my limits because I was ashamed of the pain I was causing my parents. They didn't ask me any questions about what was in my head on the day of the tragedy, why I didn't go to school that day. They didn't hold me accountable for anything, they cared for me without considering any other option. If they could do this, it would not be moral on my part to give in.

By now, it was evening, my fever had not subsided at all, I felt even worse.

'If the medication doesn't work, let's try something else. Go to the pharmacy and buy Calamine, and in the meantime, we will pack her with vinegar. Maybe she reacts better to old-fashioned cures,' the doctor said.

As if a spinal cord injury is anything like the kind of flu my great-grandmother used to treat, I thought to myself.

'Okay,' my father replied.

'I'm putting another blanket on you,' the doctor told me.

'But it will be too hot for me,' I exclaimed.

'It doesn't matter. You have to sweat to get over your fever.'

Wrapped up to my neck with a sheet and a blanket and hearing all this, I wondered how such a solution had been arrived at – my doctor's lack of experience, or the rareness of my case? My father returned with the Calamine (an old-fashioned liquid that you rub on your body), and the doctor and nurse applied Calamine all over my body and put vinegar-soaked socks on my feet, then wrapped me in another blanket.

'Good. That should help her. If her fever doesn't go down, call me. I'll be in the guard room. You can both stay during the day, but only one of you can stay at night.' – I appreciated the doctor's behaviour. Few doctors are so involved in the relationship with the patient. She may not have had much experience with cases like mine, but her kindness and involvement were boundless. Few doctors are hands on, applying vinegar and Calamine. Usually, the doctor distributes such tasks among the nurses.

'Sebi, you go to the dormitory. I'll stay with her,' my mother said.

'If you're too tired, I'll stay,' said Dad.

'It's fine. I'm staying.'

'What time is it?' I asked.

'Almost nine-thirty,' my mother answered.

'Daddy, you can go and catch the bus.'

'Don't worry about me. I'll stay with you a little longer. Do you want me to bring you something to eat in the morning? Anything you might like?'

'No, thanks.'

'Don't you want anything? Chocolate-chip cookies, pizza, anything,' my mother urged.

'No, I really don't feel like anything.'

In such moments, all your natural cravings and desires disappear. You don't need food or anything else. You only think about what is happening to you and you wait. Wait for a promise. One more word. A miracle. Anything that could make you feel better. Anything that could release you from the anxiety eating your mind and let your imagination fly to something more beautiful for a few seconds.

The night passed, but not the fever. Somehow, I was starting to become immune to it all, to endure it all. I felt passive. I didn't know how to react. I didn't need anything else. I was down but I didn't want to give up.

'I'm sorry, but we can't handle it. We will transfer her back to neurosurgery ICU,' the doctor told my father this morning.

'I understand. Thank you anyway.'

8

Back to ICU

That evening, I returned to intensive care, Mrs Lili was just starting her night shift.

'Oh my God, Alexandra! What happened? Did you misbehave?'

'Looks like I did. I think I scared them. I've had a fever since yesterday.'

'Lili and Violeta will now take care of her. They will prepare her for a spinal cord puncture, and we will run some tests, maybe we will find the cause of the fever,' the doctor on duty told my parents. 'After that, you can go in to see her for a short while.'

'Why didn't you take me to the room I was in before?' I asked Mrs Lili.

'A patient in a coma is there and it's better for you to stay away from him.'

'Why stay away? He's not dead and I'm not afraid.'

'It's not about that. He has low immunity and can get an infection at any time and pass it on. And because your body is weak, it can hurt you. We cannot put two vulnerable patients in the same ward.'

'I understand, but in the first days I stayed with that girl who was in a coma.'

'That's right, only her condition was better than that of the patient in your favourite ward.'

'Oh, oh, but how talkative you are. I'm very glad!' said Mrs Violeta, who had just entered the room with several sheets in her hand for my bed, laughing.

'Alexandra wants to be in the front room,' said Mrs Lili.

'Well, how can we do it? I know there's already someone in that room and it wouldn't be appropriate for her to be in there with him.'

'I will talk to the head nurse in the morning, I hope she comes before I leave. We could move the gentleman from there to another room, then sterilise the ward and take Alexandra there.'

'Thank you so much!' I replied happily. I felt more part of life in that room because it was positioned in such a way that I could see what was going on around me.

'Alexandra, your bed is ready, are you ready to move?' Mrs Lili asked me.

'Not really, but I have no choice!' It was scary when someone grabbed me and moved me from side to side (from stretcher to bed and vice versa). I couldn't feel my body, had no control over it, so I always felt like I would be dropped.

'Stay calm, Alexandra, no need to be scared,' insisted Mrs Violeta.

'Would we let anything bad happen to you?' said Mrs Lili.

'No, but I'm still scared.'

'We understand, Alexandra. It's normal. After all, it's physics. We understand and we think that you are the bravest!' They moved me carefully. It wasn't so bad.

'Thank you. And now what's next? I heard about some tests.'

'Yes, but before the tests, we will call the doctor to remove some fluid from your spine. Maybe that will stabilise your fever,' Mrs Lili replied.

'Will it hurt me a lot?'

'No. We will stay with you. We need to keep you on your side so the doctor can do her job. As you do not feel anything from the neck down, you will not feel the needle either.'

I got through that procedure, and now I was left with the nurse to take a sample of blood.

'I think I'll collect it from an artery, to keep the few veins left untouched for the butterfly needle,' my nurse told me. 'Do you feel sick still?'

'Somehow yes. All I want is to sleep, to feel nothing. Can you give me a sleep injection as well?'

'We won't give you diazepam tonight. We need to stabilise the fever. Looks like your secretions have gathered again. Will you allow me to do the suction? It will help you breathe better. If you want, I'll bring you an oxygen mask.'

'Okay, but I don't think I can stand too much.'

'I'll do a little, and in the morning Silviu will come to tap you. I'll give you another painkiller and we'll wait to see how you feel in an hour.'

'Okay, but I don't want to be alone.'

'You won't be alone. The doctor says your parents can come for an hour and then we will take turns. I'll be around and the doctor too. The other nurses will come and check on you. And we'll bring another patient here as soon as he comes out of surgery. We will make sure we don't leave you alone. Right now, I'll call your parents.'

I liked the time I spent with my mother and father. We talked, we ate a little, time passed very quickly, and we had to say goodbye. But only until morning when they would return to the hospital hallways. The night was incredibly difficult, but at that stage every night was difficult, and I always felt a great uneasiness.

As the nurse had told me earlier, a new roommate arrived. A man, most likely over fifty years old. He had just had surgery, I don't know where, but he wasn't allowed to get out of bed for a few hours after the operation. The nurses had tied his hands and feet to the bed. I was a little amused by his presence. As soon as the nurses left, he began to shout.

'Ma'am, ma'am!' and Mrs Lili, as she heard the noise, came.

'What happened? Are you feeling okay?'

'I feel fine, I want to get up. I want to leave. Untie me.'

'I'm afraid you have to stay still for a while. Try to calm down and be considerate. Alexandra, I haven't forgotten about you! We still have to disinfect a few wards, but when we finish, Violeta and I will come back.

'I'm fine, I was with the doctor until a few minutes ago,' I replied.

'Okay. I'm going back to work. Be good.'

'Ma'am, but I want to get up!' the gentleman from the next bed shouted again, but Mrs Lili was already gone.

'Take it easy, she'll be back soon,' I told him.

'I can't just lie here with my eyes on the ceiling. I want to get up, or at least onto my ass. Miss! Come back!'

'You have to be patient. I had a car accident three weeks ago and I can't move at all, but I still have patience. You can move, only it will hurt you if you do it now.'

'Miss! Bring an axe, ma'am, to untie these threads! Bring the axe, ma'am! Nobody hears me! I could have gone home to get an axe in the time I've been shouting. Come on, ma'am, get an axe, something, or a hatchet! Bring the axe!' he kept shouting.

Seeing that I had no one to talk to, because the man was still agitated, I said nothing more. I was silently amused by his words and I was waiting for someone to come and stay with me. One of the nurses came, not the one who had taken care of me, and she gave a tranquilliser to the poor man that calmed him down so he didn't have to make so much noise.

9

Where next?

Finally, the morning came. Some nurses came to wash me, others to give me treatment, and the doctors came on their rounds. After the rounds, Dr Popescu talked to my parents.

'I'm sorry that the Nicolina recovery hospital didn't work and you had to come back here. I've been thinking of alternative solutions. Alexandra's condition, not her physical one, but her condition as a whole, hemodynamically, is not good, especially as she still has regular fevers. We must consider a transfer to a recovery hospital which is prepared for any situation, so that Alexandra can be given the help she needs. A recovery hospital with an ICU ward. I thought, initially, of the Budimex Hospital in Bucharest, where they have recovery ward for children, but because Easter is approaching, the ward will be closed for two weeks. It's a long time to wait, two more weeks we can't waste. The Bagdasar Arseni Hospital is the other option. They have a recovery department, but it's for adults. However, I can talk to the head of the ward there and they'll take Alexandra. What do you say?'

'Two weeks plus the days of this week, so almost three weeks, is a lot. We will think about it and decide,' my father replied.

'Sure. I'm on duty today. You can come to tell me what you have decided at any time. One problem would be the very long distance to Bucharest. Being in the ambulance for that long would not be good for Alexandra. She needs a medical aeroplane equipped with everything she needs. Let's begin by filling in a form to the Bucharest air ambulance and emergency services and wait for an answer from them.'

That evening, I was moved to the front room with a gentleman who had suffered a severe stroke at work and had been severely injured. He was no longer conscious and lay completely still. The devices monitored him and only they showed the vital signs that he was still alive. My parents, sitting in the hallway, talked to his relatives and found out that he was also from Bacău.

I was overwhelmed by how many things I had learned in three weeks. I had discovered such depth of suffering that I no longer knew how to behave. I had seen cases in which patients could not even speak. Only the devices remained to speak for them. I was going through some unimaginable moments and experiences that were difficult to reproduce in words and I didn't know whether to be happy that I was still conscious and could speak, I could say, somehow, what and how I felt, or to grieve that this pain and suffering I feel will be with me forever. I will continue to carry it all, even if someday it is as memories. For the worst memories continue to summon fear even long after they are over. My entire universe had collapsed, and the crystal ball I had been spinning in until three weeks ago had been shattered into thousands of pieces. My soul shattered with it. My soul whose pieces I was trying to gather and glue back together, but which, like anything glued together, would never be the same.

For the rest of the day, my family asked about the two hospitals in Bucharest, but they didn't find out anything about the Budimex. And that's because, in fact, the doctor had not received all the updated information. The Marie Curie Children's Hospital in the Capital (formerly also called the Budimex) used to have a recovery department, but it had closed. The new Robănescu Recovery Centre has been opened in its place, located in the courtyard of the Marie Curie Hospital. I only found out about the Robănescu Children's Recovery Centre after I had arrived in Bagdasar. At the time, it was decided that I should be transferred to Bagdasar.

'Doctor, we asked around, and we think we should transfer to Bagdasar. But we would like your opinion. We will do as you think is best,' my father told the doctor.

'I think the transfer to Bagdasar is sensible. Let's wait for the answer from the air ambulances department and, depending on them, we will decide on the day of the transfer.'

In the evening, my parents stayed with me. The night passed faster, thanks to diazepam pills. In the morning, for the first time, I was hungry. I was looking forward to my family coming up with something good to eat. I kept asking Mrs Lili (not the nice one that I loved, but another nurse of the same name) when my parents would appear. Eventually they arrived, and the head nurse let my mother in.

'Good morning, baby, are you okay?' my mother asked me.

'Good morning. Why did it take you so long to come? I'm hungry! Are you starving me?' I replied angrily. I was having a nervous outburst that morning, something that had never happened before, especially for such a silly reason.

'Please forgive us. We didn't mean to be late. The first tram was crowded, and we had to wait for the next one. I will get you some food immediately,' my mother replied, while a tear rolled down her cheek.

'Sorry, I didn't mean that! I don't know what's wrong with me today.'

'Stay calm, I wasn't upset. Are you okay? Were you able to sleep?'

'I fell asleep after the injection. I have had better days, but I am okay.'

'I understand. I brought you biscuits, cherry compote and tea. I'll put them in the closet. Now, do you want Nesquik and apple strudel?'

'Yes, thank you very much.'

'You have nothing to thank me for, my love.'

'Mom, how long will it take for me to recover? What do I do about school? The tests are starting soon.'

'Don't worry, we will solve the school problem in due course. Easter is coming and soon we will leave for Bucharest to start the recovery.'

'Silviu comes to move my hands and feet, but there has been no improvement. I can't do anything alone.'

'You will be able to, don't worry. At the new hospital you will do more.'

'Good. Do you think Silviu could help me sit? Then I could see what's around me.'

'I don't think that is possible, honey, but we can talk to him.'

'I'll ask him when he comes. I'm getting terribly bored. It's all just pain, general sickness, fever, medication, shortness of breath, tapping ... I want to enjoy something or other. I want to do something new. To go out, to feel the air.'

'I know, honey, I know. We have to be patient.'

I was losing patience. It was getting harder to overcome the situation. To overcome my frustrations and look at the good side of things. It's just that I didn't see much good. And it didn't let itself be seen either. I saw nothing good in being immobilised in a bed and between four walls. I didn't see anything good in not being able to put a cup of water to my mouth. I couldn't even scratch my face. I didn't see anything good in the fact that someone was emptying my intestines, that I was incapable of even doing that. I saw absolutely nothing good. Just a lot of torment. When Silviu came, I started to shout at him.

'When will I recover?'

'There is no specific date. It depends on each patient.'

'Is there no general prognosis written in the books you learned from in college?'

'I told you, it depends on the patient and how serious the trauma is. The average would be around six months, but for some it takes longer, for others not so long.'

'What happened to me? Did a spinal break cause all these problems?'

'Well, you had a cervical spine fracture, followed by spinal cord injury. A spine fracture is not like a broken hand, you can't just put it in plaster and in a few weeks it's like new. It's more complicated.'

'So that's the meaning of the two words, spastic quadriplegia, written on the paper sheet next to the bed?'

'Yes, that is your diagnosis.'

'Can you help me sit on the edge of the bed, please?'

'Now?'

'Yes, why not?'

'I can't do it now, but I promise we'll try in the next few days. I need two more people to help.'

'Why do you need so many people?'

'You will find out the answer yourself when we lift you.'

'Okay ... can't you call those two people now? Two nurses, for example?'

'Please be patient Alexandra. I also need to talk to the doctor who operated on you. How do you feel when the bed is raised to thirty or forty degrees?'

'I can't stand it for too long. Every day the nurses raise me up, for a maximum of thirty minutes. It is even harder to breath when I am up a bit, then I get used to it, but I have some strange sensations, as if someone is squeezing my chest.'

10

Gathering drops of strength

Easter was getting closer. It was the beginning of Holy Week. Mental fatigue affected me more and more. I kept my eyes shut most of the time, trying to fall asleep. But since I hadn't been able to sleep naturally for three weeks, all I could do was keep breathing, try to calm down and imagine something beautiful.

I heard footsteps that seemed to be getting closer and closer to my bed. I opened my eyes slowly, heavily, and in front of me I saw a priest. For a moment, I thought that this was the end. Then the priest began to talk to me, He told me not to be afraid, that I was a very brave child and that he would read me a few prayers, then he would bless me. I started to be more rational, and I realised that I could still fight.

The same day, some friends and Magda visited me. I don't know if it was their idea or if my parents had asked them to, because I know that people start to forget you when you are no longer around in their day-to-day life. Anyway, I enjoyed their presence. I must have looked pretty bad, or at least very different to how they were expecting. One of my friends almost fainted when she saw me. She didn't say anything, but her face went ghostly white, and she had to sit on the edge of my bed. A nurse who was passing by told her to get up because she might give me an infection. She went out into the hall, unsteadily, apologising. She told my parents how sorry she was, and that she didn't feel good seeing me like that. I ate the pizza that my friends had brought all the way from Bacău because I had told them that I wanted a pizza from a certain pizzeria there. After they left, I fell asleep without any pills or injections for the first time. This was even a surprise for the nurses. It happened because the power of God is above everything. I felt better, even rested.

In the evening, my father, then my mother took turns with me. Before the accident I was very careful with my hygiene and appearance, but in the recent weeks, all my attention had been focused on survival. Every morning, the nurses washed my face with a cloth, but now I felt the need for more than that. That evening I found a way to brush my teeth, with a toothbrush and toothpaste – just like normal life.

'Daddy, how good it is to sleep! I had almost forgotten that feeling,' I told my father.

'I am so happy for you, darling. Do you want me to get you something to eat or buy you anything in particular?'

'No, thank you, I'm not really hungry, but I would like something else...'

'Tell me?'

'I would like to brush my teeth with a toothbrush, in a normal way.'

My father smiled. 'There should be a toothbrush and toothpaste around here. I brought them earlier, with the napkins. Here they are, found them! But how would you like us to do this? I don't want it to make you sick.'

'Well ... first you have to take the remote control by the bed and lift my torso until I tell you to stop.'

'And which one is the button?'

'Try them one by one,' I said laughing.

'No,' he laughed too. 'Let's do this logically, according to the drawings. Here it is. I'll start pressing and you tell me when to stop.'

'Stop! That's good. Come closer and tell me if you can reach my mouth.'

'Yes, that's good for me. That should be okay, you are okay, right?'

'Yes. It takes me a while to get used to sitting up, then I feel better. Please can you get a cup of water, a straw, lots of napkins and a toothbrush?'

'Ok. Tell me how to do it so I don't hurt you.'

'Be careful. I'll open my mouth and you brush slowly, using the same movements as when you brush your teeth. Then, give me water with a straw, I'll rinse and spit it into the cup. We can do that twice. Then, wipe me with the wipes or, better, with a wet wipe and then with a dry one. Sound good?'

Although I was living in an extreme situation, I had managed not to lose hope. It's really hard to depend on others for everything. I believed that it was only a temporary situation, which would soon return to normal. Because of this, I agreed to endure everything that was happening to me. Even though I couldn't do anything, I was glad that those around me were happy to help me do the things I could not – it certainly helped my mood. This was the case with the teeth brushing. I was so happy that my father managed to fulfil this wish. A desire that seems so insignificant for all those who see brushing their teeth as a routine. But brushing your teeth with your own hands is such a great thing!

Later, around eleven p.m., when everything had seemed to calm down, the man in the next bed suddenly became sick. His monitoring equipment made a louder noise than usual. The nurses arrived immediately and gave him emergency treatment.

One stayed by my side to distract me. The man started to vomit and to make strange noises. I had never heard a noise from him since we'd been together in the room. Not a sound. A cry. A sigh. Nothing at all. He was unconscious after the stroke he had suffered. Every day, his family sat by him, especially his wife, who was visibly upset by the situation. She looked at him, waiting for him to wake up. Eventually, the nurses stabilised and intubated him.

'Alexandra, are you okay?' one of the nurses asked me.

'I am. What about the man?'

'Let's hope he gets well too. I understand that today you managed to fall asleep. Bravo! I am very happy for you.'

'Yes, I know! I don't want the sleeping injection tonight. I don't want to get addicted to them. Maybe I can fall asleep again. Will you stay and make sure the man is okay?'

'Don't worry. We'll move him to another ward tomorrow. Try to stay calm and not think about him and what you heard. Don't be afraid, okay?'

'I am not afraid; I feel sorry for him – what he's going through.'

'What can we do? We each have a fate, Alexandra. Stay calm, okay? Good night, Alexandra!'

'God, how much suffering you have left on earth!' I said to myself. The situation of the man in the room affected me, but somehow it gave me another drop of strength. Power, because I still had some part of me left. My brain was untouched. I remained the centre of my actions, even if my body could no longer perform most of them. I had the power to think, see and speak. I had more than my ward neighbour. And for this reason, but also for others, I had no right to give up.

11

Daily rhythms

The next day, I had a new roommate. Her name was Simona. She was a young woman of no more than thirty years old. She could move, she could walk, but she couldn't breathe very well; she suffocated suddenly for no reason, then panicked. I was glad that I finally had company day and night.

After the one p.m. doctor's visit, Ana-Maria came by. She was a lovely lady whose mother had suffered a stroke and was in the hospital. My parents had befriended her and her husband. Sometimes, in the evening, they would drive my parents to the dormitory where they slept, so that they didn't have to depend on the tram or the bus.

'Alexandra, we are going home to Bârlad. My mother is better. It was great meeting you.' We exchanged phone numbers to keep in touch. 'Maybe we'll meet again. Your parents are extraordinary people, and you are a very brave and strong girl. Don't give up! I'm sure you'll get better soon!' – After a long time, I found out that, in fact, "my mother is better" meant that she died, and they told me that only so as not to burden me with further negative information.

Perhaps when you die, you really get better. You have no more pain. Nothing hurts you anymore. Maybe you're just happy and that's it.

That evening, my godparents came to see me. I didn't know they were coming. My mother only told me when they arrived in the hospital hallway. When I saw them, I started to cry. It was not a normal cry, but a hysterical one. I couldn't control myself or talk – I felt so overwhelmed. Even the ECG went crazy and made a lot of noise. A nurse came to see what had happened.

'Alexandra, what is it? Relax. You will faint, breathe! Are you in pain? Does anything bother you? Look, you have visitors. You always enjoy visitors.'

'I can't control myself,' I said trembling.

'Don't panic. Nothing will happen to you! I'll give you a little nasal oxygen, you focus on breathing.'

After a few minutes I recovered and started talking to my godparents. They are always such a warm and pleasant presence. They have two daughters: Renata and Andreea Alexandra, who has the same name as me. I think this is where my parents got the inspiration from when they chose my first name. When I was younger and I went to see them; I played with Reni and her toy babies. Sometimes we argued over them. Later, when I was older, she showed me her makeup kit from the "Secret of Sabrina" collection. Each time I saw her she had collected more makeup and the kit's container soon became too small. Once, she did my makeup. What memories!

'Are you on your second dish now?' joked my godfather with a smile on his face and looking at the drip.

'Yes, it's over. Now for dessert. I hope it's something with cream and chocolate,' I replied laughing.

After over an hour the nurse appeared again.

'I'm sorry, but you will have to leave now.'

'Sure, thank you for letting us see her!' my godfather replied.

'Andruţo, be strong. Don't let anyone knock you down.' said my godmother.

'We are by your side, and we are waiting for your return home! We love you so much.'

After the visitors left, I talked to Simona until our evening treatment. I asked for diazepam, because I had not been able to fall asleep and I felt the need for a break. I fell asleep instantly. I didn't even have time to say goodnight to Simona.

'Alexandra, I called out for you several times last night, but you didn't answer me. I wasn't feeling well and I wanted to talk,' Simona told me in the morning.

'I'm sorry, Simona. I can't hear anything while I'm sleeping because of the injection and I probably only wake up when it loses its effect.'

Meanwhile, the emergency air ambulance services in Bucharest responded positively to the request made by my parents. On the third day of Easter, they scheduled a flight to bring some organs to Timisoara. They said they would pick me up on the return journey and take me to Bucharest, to the Bagdasar Hospital.

'I understand that you are leaving for Bucharest next week?' the nurse who came for my lunch treatment asked me.

'Yes ...' I answered not very excited.

'I'm glad for you! You don't seem excited, but you should be – it's part of your recovery process.'

'I got used to you and the people here.'

'And you will find good people to get along with in Bucharest.'

'Hopefully.'

'Look at this – the butterfly needle is upset too.'

'Is it clogged?'

'Yes. I only had one more syringe to give you, but it doesn't work anymore. I'll have to change it.'

'Charge yourself with patience. In fact, you have to be patient.'

'I have patience. Not a problem. And you're dear to me anyway, and we're still talking while I do it.'

'Can you put me in a purple flyer, please?'

'I'll try, but your veins don't want to. Typical! The needle bent!'

While I was telling her things about myself, and she was looking for my lucky vein, another nurse slipped her head through the door.

'Come, please! Mr Popescu is in a hurry.'

How subtly and delicately she said it. But I already understood. It was about the man I was in the room with the day before. The man from Bacău. He was hurrying to a place considered by specialists to be better. A place where, they say, there is no pain, suffering or wickedness. But he hurried too soon. He would have had a lot more time. It's just that it was not up to him. Somewhere up there, that's how it was scheduled.

All our lives we run around seeking material things and we very rarely realise what really matters. We realise when it is too late. And we only do that when we lose something or a loved one. Sometimes it is not even enough to lose someone, because we are so concerned about wealth that the soul becomes a negligible thing.

12

The gift of being able to sit up

'What are you girls doing?' asked Silviu, the physiotherapist, as he entered the ward.

'We are chatting so that time passes!' Simona replied.

'Do you have any surprises for us?' I joked.

'In fact, I do for you, Alexandra – I'm going to call your parents and a nurse to get you up on the edge of the bed. As I promised you.'

I had been waiting for this moment for a long time. I was expecting an improvement. One more step forward. Something good to give me a boost so that I could keep hope. But it was disappointing. It was the second sign that helped me understand that my situation was worse than I thought.

First, Silviu put on my cervical collar. Then, the nurse pulled my legs to the edge of the bed, my father grabbed me from the left, and Silviu from the right and they gathered me up. There was nothing I could do. I couldn't even hold my head. It was pushed against the collar, falling slightly on Silviu's shoulder. I tried to roll my eyes in as many directions as I could, to see what was around me. I only managed to be up for about thirty seconds, then my eyes went black. My ears blocked, my breath cut off, and my voice disappeared. I barely managed to articulate a few sounds to make it clear that I was sick.

After that, my morale was really low. I couldn't sit on my ass or even be held by three people. I was experiencing a thousand feelings. Especially feelings of revolt. However, I did not give up. I tried that lift a second time, and a third time, but it was just as bad.

The night of the Resurrection, Mrs Lili was on duty – not Mrs Lili who was dearest to me, but the other Mrs Lili. She brought a lighted candle to our room. All I could see was the hospital strip lights and the candle. It felt rather sinister image. Scenarios were playing though my head – mostly related to death. I didn't understand the point of surviving the accident if life was only to be suffering and struggling and causing pain to those around me. I couldn't understand how God, who – I was told as a child – loved children, could let a child go through so much. I was trying to think of all the diseases I knew of, especially cancer, and to compare their symptoms and repercussions with all the symptoms I had. I couldn't because none of them seemed comparable to my own. It was too much. When you are ill you have certain problems and pains, but you still have something left. You can still make a gesture. For me, nothing worked. My whole body was affected. Everything had been taken from me when I was less than fourteen years old. The age which is said to be the most beautiful period of life. But I was never going to experience it.

13

Transfer to Bucharest

The first and second days of Easter passed quickly. Several relatives came to see me. The plan was for me to leave for Bucharest on the third day of Easter. In the morning, Mrs Lili and my mother washed and dressed me in some new white pyjamas. My parents gathered all their belongings from the dormitory where they had been staying for the last month. They put their bags in my uncle's car. He had driven from Bacau to help with the move. After packing, my father and my uncle came to the hospital to collect the few things that belonged to me. They stayed until the afternoon then said goodbye. The first stop was to Bacău, to change their thick, winter clothes to lighter, more seasonal ones. Of course, this operation took quite a long time, and it wasn't until around seven p.m. that they left for Bucharest.

Shortly after seven p.m., the crew from the emergency department arrived and took my mother and me to the airport. I was a little agitated and somehow afraid of what was to come. On the one hand, I told myself that the sun would soon come out on my street, but on the other hand I was disheartened. Almost a month had passed, and my situation had not improved much.

'I'm not going on the plane!' I said when the medical crew took me out of the ambulance and were about to take me to the plane.

It was my first time flying and I was full of emotions; in a state of fear and wishing that my first plane flight could be normal, in a normal chair and in a normal situation. Not on a stretcher, with belts, with my hands and feet tied so they would not fall during the flight and get hurt. Not without any feelings or motor activity from the neck down. Not with wounds and scars all over my body.

The plane began to take off, I tried to distract myself. I don't know what a person without problems feels when flying, but I didn't really feel anything. I could see nothing but the plane's shell above me.

'How long does it take to get there?' I asked.

'About an hour.'

'Mommy, my hair is in my eyes, and I need a napkin.'

'I can take your hair out from your eyes. Your mother can't reach you,' replied the nurse who was closer to me – I was accompanied by a doctor and a nurse.

'Thank you. And a napkin. I have to spit.' After all the secretion suctions from my throat and nose, the ICU people advised me not to swallow saliva but to spit it out so that the secretions could not build up. Theoretically, they could be removed more easily if I could cough, but since I couldn't, I had to be aspirated so I wouldn't drown in my saliva, so I had developed the habit of always spitting.

'Right away.'

They didn't want me bothering them during the flight, so "right away" didn't mean "I'll give you a napkin right away", but rather "I'll immediately put something in your vein to shut you up". I woke up when we landed. The team took me from the airport by ambulance. This time, the medical crew consisted of women. They turned on the siren, and in about thirty minutes I was in front of Bagdasar Hospital. I felt very strange on the way,

I wanted to vomit. When they got me out of the ambulance, I felt a little better. It was dark outside and around ten p.m. It took about forty minutes for me to be admitted to the hospital. Then I was taken up to the tenth floor, to the recovery section, where the doctor was waiting for me. My mother signed a few more papers before they took me to the room they had prepared. When I entered, I could see the TV on the wall from the stretcher – I was so happy. Immediately two nurses came and put me to bed.

'Wow!' was my response when they took off my collar, so I could turn my head from side to side and see my new surroundings.

I was in a room with two beds, one for me and the other for my mother. The beds were arranged in such a way that you could see everything in the room. The TV was flat and had multiple channels. I asked my mother to turn it to cartoons. I had missed them so much! The bedclothes were not white, like in a hospital, but yellow. The living room was beautifully arranged. If I had seen it in a picture, I would have mistaken it for a hotel room. Between the beds, next to the bedside tables, was a table and two chairs. On the wall to my left was a beautiful painting. Next to my mother's bed, a vertical mirror. The room was also equipped with a private bathroom, air conditioning, a small refrigerator (like a minibar) and a closet. Too bad the beautiful dream didn't last long. In the following days I was going to find out that "living" in that room cost a hundred euros per day, and was therefore intended for those with connections and money.

'Do you like it, Andreea?' my mother asked me.

'It is so beautiful. Can you cover me up, please? I don't feel that cold feeling, but I'm shaking. Let's call my father,' I said through gritted teeth, the tremor intensifying.

'We'll call him, just calm down a little, so you don't scare him. You have cold feet, maybe this is where the tremor is coming from. I'll pop a blanket on you.'

My father and my uncle arrived after midnight. They came to the hospital to check we were okay, then went straight to the dormitory to sleep. They came back in the morning. Uncle stayed until noon, when we said goodbye and he left for home.

14

The new hospital

At first glance, it seemed to be a great recovery department, compared to Nicolina Hospital. The beds were the same as those in the ICU, with remote control and anti-pressure sore mattresses, and the nurses were experienced in caring for and handling an immobilised person in bed. Two nurses came to take tests for infection, then I met the director of the hospital and the head of the recovery department, Mr Professor Doctor, or Professor (as most people called him) Onose Gelu.

The meeting with the professor was memorable and especially constructive.

After about twenty years of treating patients with severed spinal cords, a car accident brought the professor into hospital in a wheelchair. To treat patients with central vertebral trauma, traumatic brain injury and other traumas or conditions that require neuro-psychomotor recovery for half of your medical career, and then to become a patient yourself in the ward you run, is quite something. It's more than the irony of fate. But he fought on and today he is a model of strong will for his patients, as he was for me.

The professor was candid and direct in front of my parents, especially in front of my father, who he had most of the discussions with.

'Ten per cent of her movement, that's all she will recover. Medicine has its limits and until it evolves, we do not have a cure for spinal cord injuries,' were the words of the Professor in one discussion with my father. No matter how crazy, harsh or insensitive my parents thought him at the time, today he has all their respect, and mine, even though it took me a while to come to this position. I realise that his prognosis had no tinge of malice; he only meant to portray reality.

Because I still had a fever, I went through several investigations and ultrasounds, and the next day, the professor called a doctor from plastic surgery to look at my left hand. It was decided that I needed more operations, without delay. I was scheduled for the first operation three days later. All the doctors prescribed me tablets, so it was time for me to learn to take the pills lying down in bed.

'How can I take all these pills?' I asked my parents.

'We will find a way,' my father replied.

'Now let's eat and see what we can do with the pills,' said my mother.

Mrs Laura, the physiotherapist, who was passively mobilising my upper and lower limbs, treated me only briefly because her contract was finishing. After that, she left Mr Max in charge of the physiotherapy. Mr Max talked to my parents about my condition and instructed them to order me a wheelchair so that I could be wheeled to the physiotherapy room, where there were several devices that could help me. I needed a chair adapted to my needs. A chair with an adjustable backrest because I couldn't withstand being at ninety degrees. And more importantly a high back, specially adapted for those who cannot even hold their head up, like me. Ramona, my cousin, researched the best options in consultation with Mr Max. In the end, she ordered one from a company in Spain. It took about a month for the chair to arrive, but in the end that didn't matter as I couldn't have sat or stayed in it any earlier.

Eventually, I managed to get used to swallowing the pills lying down in bed, and sometimes when I felt able to, I took them with my torso raised to about thirty-five degrees. I had to take seven pills in the morning, seven at noon and another ten in the evening, plus some syrups and other medicines dissolved in water. I drank more than half a litre of water for one lot. I could barely refrain from vomiting, but as I believed the pills would make me recover, I gritted my teeth and moved on. The breathing problem had improved, in the sense that I could breathe better without having episodes of suffocation. The most gratifying thing that had kept me from losing hope was that I had some sensitivity on one side of my right arm. I could feel it when someone touched my arm, up to my elbow. It wasn't a normal, uniform sensibility, but the fact that it existed made me very happy. I even managed to tense my triceps a little. Although these new feelings didn't help me much and I still couldn't move the limb, I considered it progress.

15

'Stop bothering people'

After about two days, I went down to the ninth floor to the plastic surgery department for the first operation on my left hand. The hospital rooms there were not so nice. There were fewer facilities, and I had to stay with two other people in the room. The night after the operation, both my parents stayed with me. I was sick and in a terrible state. I started to cry, I didn't want anything, I couldn't cope with anything and couldn't stand it anymore; I was very agitated. That night was terribly hard, in the morning it felt as if a week had passed. Before the doctors' morning rounds, a lady, who was mobile, could eat, drink, walk – that is, she was much better off than me – had complained to the doctors that I had given a "performance" last night and that she could not rest. A nurse told my parents to leave the room until the doctors' rounds were over.

'Miss, you are not at a hotel here. I understand you're making a lot of noise and bothering everyone. You're not the only patient here. Please stop fussing so much and calm down!' one of the doctors told me sharply.

'You cannot scream all night. You must have respect for those around you,' added another doctor.

I didn't say anything at the time. I was frozen. I think my soul was paralysed, as well as my body. No matter how bad it has been in the last month, I had not felt as demoralised as I did in those moments. The sky was falling on my head. That was the moment that triggered my mental collapse. I had lost all trace of strength, patience and understanding. How can you, as a doctor, tell me I'm pampered and fussy? To me, to a child, who has not been able to move at all for more than a month, and no longer feels anything from the neck down, is turned around in a sheet and emptied by someone else. How can you be a doctor and behave in this way? After the doctors left, I burst into tears, a terrible wrenching cry. My soul hurt from the way I had become, and I no longer knew how to behave.

'Andreea, what happened? What did they tell you?' my parents asked me, probably believing that the doctors had told me the truth about my condition.

'They scolded me for crying and making a noise last night. They think I'm pretending, but I can't cope anymore. An idiot doctor told me not to be fussy anymore,' I sobbed.

'The idiot doctor is right here and is the same "idiot" who operated on your hand,' the person in the doorway replied as soon as she heard my outcry, then left.

I had no idea that she had operated on me, but even so, I was not sorry that I called her an idiot because her behaviour was unfair and unkind. However, in time, we became friends. She showed humanity and took care of my hand. However, this discussion had also reached the ears of Professor Onose, who was very disturbed by my attitude and almost wiped the floor with my parents. In his opinion I had to end with the fussiness. This is always the case; outsiders can never understand you. Many just criticise and misjudge you.

I stayed in the plastic surgery department for a few more days, then my condition worsened. I felt worse and worse, I couldn't even eat, and my fever couldn't be controlled. The decision was made to transfer me to the infectious diseases hospital. But while I was in the surgery ward, I had some other memorable experiences. They called in a psychiatrist, probably because the whole medical body was tired of hearing me cry, and the best way to silence a person is with drugs prescribed by a psychiatrist.

'What are these pills for?' I asked the doctor.

'To make you smile more!' she answered. That is, to fool me and silence me, to make me numb, to simply make me forget about myself. In general, this is what most treatments prescribed by a psychiatrist do. Such drugs do not treat the cause, they only prolong it. The pills made me drowsy and I couldn't think anymore. Don't imagine that I slept well: I slept terribly, I didn't feel rested. Sleep caused by pills is not the same as a normal night's sleep. I was in constant torment.

16

The difference between living and existing

On May 1st, they transferred me to the hospital for infectious diseases. I have never seen so much indifference and disrespect. It took more than nine hours for an ambulance to come from one sector of the city to another to take me to the other hospital. I had been on a stretcher for the whole day waiting to go and I was in an unimaginable state. I wondered how I was still conscious, but the doctors did not care. They just shrugged, and when my parents asked them why it was taking so long for an ambulance to pick me up, they would respond with the famous words, "Be patient!"

But how much patience do you have when you see your child being destroyed by helplessness? My parents were also at the end of their tether, they were so close to collapsing. My uncle and aunt arrived from Bacău, and the ambulance had still not arrived. My aunt decided to take matters into her own hands.

'Ma'am, listen here! Why are you messing about with this child? We have just driven three hundred kilometres, and in that time an ambulance can't even make it from one side of the city to another? You have kept these people in agony since this morning. I don't know what you are playing at, but if the ambulance doesn't show up in half an hour, I promise there will be trouble!'

Less than fifteen minutes after my aunt's "discussion" with the head nurse, the ambulance appeared in front of the hospital, because that's how it is here. Until you make a scene, you don't get anywhere. People prefer aggression to good words, and things rarely happen out of solidarity and respect.

The ambulance ride to the hospital was torturous for me, mentally speaking. Although the driver was not going more than fifty kilometres per hour, it felt too fast, and I thought I would fall off the stretcher. All sorts of scenarios were running through my mind: we were going to have an accident; we were going to overturn and die – all sorts of negative things. I was afraid of everything. After a lot of stress and tears, we arrived at the new hospital. I couldn't see much except that the hospital was surrounded by a lot of trees. As with any admission procedures, I waited until the necessary documents were completed, then I was taken to a ward.

It was a very small room; all the equipment was crowded in with barely space to move around it. The facilities left much to be desired. The hospital bed was not at all suitable for a patient with spinal cord injury. I was lucky to have the pressure-sore mattress my father bought me when I stayed at Nicolina's, because otherwise it would have been a tragedy. It should be appreciated, however, that in the room there was a TV, basic, but at least it was there. When I was moved to the new bed, the nurses practically jumped on me. They changed my catheter and did several medical procedures with various solutions, then – without exaggerating – they took at least half a litre of blood, in different containers, for analysis.

I spent three weeks in the infectious diseases unit, during which time I received dozens of ampoules of antibiotics, in an attempt to stabilise and improve my condition. The test results were inconclusive. Most values were well below the normal threshold. The doctors did everything they could and tested my reaction to several treatments, until they found one that seemed to have an effect. To keep me stable, they took my blood every other day until my right hand and legs were full of marks, and the nurses could barely insert a butterfly needle. My sense of taste and smell disappeared from all the medication. Since I could no longer feel the taste of the food or smell it, I had no desire to eat anything.

As if it wasn't enough that I couldn't feel my body, now I really didn't feel anything. I had reached that phase where I only existed, I no longer lived, because there is a huge difference between existing and living.

'Good morning sunshine! How are you doing?' the doctor asked me entering the room. The doctor who took care of my case was an upright woman and a dedicated doctor. She had a warm presence and always had a smile on her face. 'How is your sense of taste doing? You still haven't eaten anything?'

'The same. I can't eat when I'm like this, it's useless.'

'I brought you these bottles for you to drink. They are supplements that I hope will give at least a five per cent improvement, but you will have to help us too. You must eat something, anything. The longer that you don't eat the harder it will be for your body. What we administer to your veins is not sufficient if you do not also have some food.'

'I'll try.'

'I'll prescribe you an oral solution with glycerine, maybe that will improve your taste.'

It was a tough three weeks. Since this was a hospital for infectious diseases, the medical staff did not know how to deal with my needs. Nobody knew how to turn me with the sheet from side to side. Only one nurse had some knowledge in the field because she had worked in a ward where people were bedridden. This meant that my parents had to adapt to the situation and learn to turn me from side to side and do my personal hygiene.

Of course, it wasn't easy. I screamed every time someone touched and moved me, and they were always afraid they would hurt me. Theoretically, they were meant to change my body position every four hours, but in practice, it only happened once a day. Some days I didn't let them move me at all. I could only bear lying on my back or on my right side, because my left hand had been freshly operated on, and a skin graft had been taken from my leg for my hand, if I moved too much, it would bleed. After three or four days, the doctor who operated on me came to bandage my hand. I didn't want to see my hand. I said I would wait until it healed and the bandages had been removed, thinking about the words of the ICU doctor, that my hand would look the same as before.

During these three weeks, my parents asked Mr Max, the physiotherapist from Bagdasar, to come and mobilise my limbs, so that I would not have muscle retractions. Mr Max was a good and honest man, and I have always appreciated him. At fifty-five years old with a Bucharest accent, he had a pure soul, and it was clear that he liked his chosen profession even after so many years.

'Tell me, Andreea, how are you?' Mr Max asked me one afternoon as he mobilised my lower right limb.

'I do not know anymore. Tell me, when will I recover? When will I go? When will I be able to put my hand on my face? When will I be able to scratch myself? When will I be able to bring a cup of water to my mouth?'

'Andreea, you have to fight and work for it. Don't imagine that one morning you will wake up and get out of bed all of a sudden, because it won't happen. You must pull yourself together and do everything you can to be well. You have to eat and fight not to give up. Understand?'

'Yes ... I think I understand, it's just so hard.'

'If you want to emerge victorious from this, push yourself. By the way, I talked to your cousin. The wheelchair will arrive soon.'

'Yes, I heard that. When I return to Bagdasar, will you put me in it?'

'Sure. Just fight to get better, to get back in good shape so that you can get out of here and continue your recovery.'

After three weeks with only a few hours' sleep and constant fatigue, my parents had become two heroes. They did not complain about anything but were visibly marked by the situation and changed. There were days when they did shifts, my father staying with me during the day and my mother at night, so that they could cope. They couldn't rest either, always thinking of me, but the mere fact that they were taking a shower at the dormitory or going out of the hospital, out of that painful environment, meant a lot. It was a way for them to recharge their batteries.

I was not so heroic; I was aware of everything that was happening around me and I was tired of absolutely everything. My psyche was deteriorating day by day. Almost two months had gone by since I landed in bed, immobilised, unable to make any further gestures. I hadn't gone mad, but there was so much pain accumulating every day that I couldn't find anything to enjoy.

17

The feeling of falling

'Do you still have that little mirror with you?' I asked my mother.

'I think so. Why?'

'I want to see my face. I haven't looked in a mirror for almost two months and I want to see what I look like. Please could you find the mirror and hold it so I can see myself.'

'Okay, let's see if I can find it.' She hesitated at first, then at my insistence she did as I asked. Holding it up she asked, 'Is it okay like this? Can you see yourself?'

I was shocked by the reflection that greeted my eyes. 'I look ... I look horrible! I'm so ugly. I'm covered in spots, my eyebrows are huge, they don't even have a shape, my face is dry, my lips are cracked. I don't look like that!' I shouted, bursting into tears.

'Calm down, you are still beautiful! Don't cry, please,' my mother replied, tears streaming down her cheeks.

'What can we do? I can't stand it anymore; I don't mean anything anymore!'

'Don't say that; you are going to be fine. Tomorrow, Uncle, Aunt and Ramo will come. I'll talk to them and ask them to bring a pair of tweezers, what do you think?'

'Okay, but it's not enough. My head is itching and I'm tired of everything.'

'I will go out to look for some dry shampoo and try to comb your hair as best as I can, from the position you are in, but please my darling, don't cry anymore.'

After a lot of effort from my mother to calm me down, I gave in and stopped crying. I began to look for something on TV that would distract me. I was being very difficult and certainly very hard to bear. The nights were a heavy burden, their passage dark and overwhelming. I didn't sleep much, and I always felt the need for someone to sit next to me. Every night my mother sat on a chair by my bed, talking and encouraging me. Some nights, to keep my mind busy, my mother would read various crosswords to me, and I would search for the right answer. The spasms, those involuntary, uncontrolled movements of my lower limbs, had intensified and I was perpetually in fear that they might throw me out of bed. It may seem hard to imagine, but those movements appeared whenever they wanted and were increasingly aggressive. The knee jumps up and then drops or the whole limb trembles. The fact that these things were happening, and I had no control over them at all, frustrated me enormously.

Sometimes, I managed to fall asleep during the day, in the hours when I was turned on the right side, but even then, it was very difficult for me. In the first days at the hospital, I screamed and cried in fear and pain. I did not feel the pain in a particular place, but the sort that ran across my whole body. My fear was caused by helplessness. I was continually afraid of falling even though I was supported by several pillows. Most of the nurses were afraid to come to me, probably because they didn't know how to deal with me. I talked to a psychologist every day, but mentally I didn't make much improvement. My morale was still very low.

Later in the week Uncle, Aunty and Ramo came to see me. They brought food for me and my parents because my parents were also barely eating. Just before they arrived, I spoke to Magda on the phone.

'Andreea, some pictures of you from the hospital appeared on Facebook,' Magda told me.

'What do you mean? What pictures?' I was shocked.

'Some pictures where you are bandaged around your neck and it is clear that you can barely breathe. There is an appeal for a fundraiser.'

'What? No! Who posted them?'

'I have no idea! Someone has made a page for you, I don't know who is behind it, but I thought you should know.'

'I want to report them, maybe they will take it down. This is awful. Thanks for telling me.'

I then found out that it was my cousin, Ramona, who had posted the pictures and started raising funds. I was furious with her. I cried, I screamed at her and scolded her. I felt humiliated that people should see me like this. Eventually I realised I was wrong. She just wanted to help me. So many people had to help me which meant a lot of money was spent on me every day and that requires even more help. Many acquaintances and strangers became involved in those days.

After I calmed down, my father and Ramo stayed with me and fed me some meat puree while my mother went out in the hospital courtyard with my uncle and aunt. It was one of the few days when I managed to eat something.

'Come on, Emma, get in the car to eat a bowl of soup,' Aunty told my mother.

'Right away, dear, but first I need to make a phone call to that horrible girl.'

My mother was referring to Magda. She was bothered that she had told me about the pictures, so she got on the phone and called Magda's father. As she never liked him, I imagine that the discussion was not filled with sweet words.

The fundraising continued. Ramona even organised a charity concert. At such moments you realise who your true friends are. There were people whom I could have sworn were friends, but who turned their backs on me in those moments. However, there were also people for whom I did not give two pennies, but who turned out to be there for me. I was filled with gratitude. In such moments you also experience situations that leave you speechless. Ramona had received a phone call from an old man who told her that he had found out about my case from the newspaper and wanted to give me some money. She was sceptical at first, but then she put her fear aside and went to the address indicated by the old man. There she learnt a real life lesson. She found a man from that rare category of person. Those who are seemingly simple, but rich in soul. A person who does not even have enough for themself, but whose soul is upset when they notice the need in the eyes of the other. A person who shares their little with those around them. These are people who deserve all our respect. People who enjoy the happiness of others and for whom well-being is not defined by something physical, but by something that comes from within, from the soul.

18

Fight for yourself

By the end of May, after three weeks spent at the Dr Victor Babeș infectious diseases hospital, I was transferred back to Bagdasar, to the recovery department, where I stayed until 1st July. Initially the return to Bagdasar was hard. I was very weak when I returned to the recovery department, and the doctors were extremely reserved and sharp.

On one particularly difficult day, Professor Onose spoke to my father in no uncertain terms.

'Mr Lichi, our body consists of input and output processes. If Alexandra doesn't try harder to help herself, she will die. That is a fact. We're done with the fussiness and while I understand she is going through shock, you have a duty to be more direct with her and not spare her. She needs to understand the situation she is in and try harder to recover. Stop comforting her so much. I had another case with a young woman who refused to try, and her parents simply left her alone for six months so that she would confront reality. I'm not urging you to leave, but you have to allow Alexandra to understand certain things. We are doing what we can, the rest depends on her.'

At that point, when the doctor told me I was not trying hard enough, I felt like I did not even have the strength to breathe. It was painful to hear. In some ways I wanted everything to end because I had already endured too much, but something in me knew I could not give up entirely.

The wheelchair was about to arrive from Spain and the next stage of the rehabilitation about to begin. Recently, my upper right arm had showed signs of healing. I was able to move my arm and forearm so I could bring the limb to my stomach. It seemed like significant progress, although in practice it didn't help that much. I could move my arm and forearm, but they were limited movements. I couldn't move my fingers, so I couldn't do anything practical with the progress I had made. Nonetheless, it boosted my morale, especially when I received encouragement from the medical staff.

Some mornings later, Professor Onose came to me. 'Hey little kitten, you shouldn't stay disabled like me, you must work with us and fight for your body! I'm going to a conference abroad for a few weeks, and Dr H. will take care of you. I understand that the wheelchair will arrive soon and I hope this will motivate you because it is a big step to recovery. You will not live lying flat, the chair will make it easier for you to sit up and move around.'

The presence of the professor was extremely motivating. Although he was in a wheelchair, he was extremely active. He was an inspiration for us, the patients who listened to him and watched him. He was harsh, at least that's how I perceived it at first, then I realised that the harshness reflected the reality, and it was not in his character to give people false hope. I liked that he was honest and encouraged me as he knew best, but I didn't understand what he meant when he told me I shouldn't stay like him. I thought he was referring to a period of a few months until I recovered and was in a better position than him – in fact he was referring to the long term. Medicine is continuously evolving, and the professor hoped that I might live to see a treatment developed for central vertebral traumas.

However, we were not at that stage yet. The days were boring and monotonous – very few hours of sleep, fatigue, torment and pain. Endless pills, tests and ampoules into the butterfly needle, absent taste, and turning every four hours. Staying in the hospital was also extremely expensive. Hundreds of lei were spent every day on medicines. We had to buy most of the drugs, the injections and IV drip, even the injections in my stomach to prevent blood clotting.

Every morning Mr Max came for the physiotherapy session. All the movements were passive, except for my right arm, where I managed to actively flex and extend my elbow; otherwise he mobilised every joint. At the end of physio class, I practiced sitting on the edge of the bed held on all sides. There was no real improvement since my last attempt to sit up on the ICU ward. The same sickness and nausea swelled in me, my vision would darken, and I could no longer speak.

'This is not at all good. You should be in a wheelchair by now. We need to find a way to keep you from blacking out. Keep the bed at forty-five degrees for as long as you can every day,' Mr Max told me.

'I'm doing that already. Not all day – but the bed is raised. The nurses leave my torso higher even when I am on one side,' I replied.

'Theoretically, today is my last day of work, before the holidays, but I am not satisfied. Keep your torso up for as long as you can today, and I will come in tomorrow, just for you, to practice sitting on the edge of the bed. The day after tomorrow I will come again and put you in the chair. You may not be able to withstand the backrest at ninety degrees, but at least at seventy-five. Let's get you out of this bed at least. Don't you want that?'

'Of course I do, yes! But what if it gets worse?'

'Eh, come on! Stop thinking like that. In the worst case, you will faint, but we will wake you up. We can slap you,' he replied with a laugh.

'Good, good. I trust you,' I added, smiling.

'One more thing, start eating properly.'

The rest of that day was better. I even managed to eat, and not just anything. I wanted pizza. My father knew that there was a pizzeria at a subway station, so he brought me one from there, a pizza with mozzarella and ham. Towards the evening Andrena a young woman who was in the hospital due to a car accident, came to my room. She brought me a box of chocolates.

A few days before, when I was very low the nurses brought Andrena to meet me and keep me talking. She had several spinal fractures, but now she was moving in a wheelchair, as I was going to do, though she was further ahead. Her upper limbs were not affected, nor her legs, and she was moving. Soon she would be able to stand again. She had also had her accident in March. She was with her boyfriend, who lost control of the steering wheel and drove into a bridgehead. He died instantly, she remained to fight on. Their accident had taken place near a restaurant, where a wedding was taking place. Many people had gathered around the car, someone even wanted to take them out of the pile of metal, but an enlightened mind opposed and did not let anyone touch them until the medical crew came.

That is why it would be good to have medical education in schools, so that people might know more about prevention. In my case, the woman who pulled me out of the car caused further damage because she had minimal knowledge about what should be done. A victim of a car accident should never be touched. If you really want to help, see if the victim is aware and talk to them, but don't touch them, as it can do more harm than good and crush their last chances of survival. Even if a fire breaks out, use a fire extinguisher and wait for the ambulance.

19

The wheelchair

I waited impatiently for the next two days to pass, for the special Sunday when I would use the wheelchair for the first time. It was a difficult psychological threshold to digest. At thirteen years old, to be in the position of having to depend on an object to move. Wheelchairs were objects that until two months ago, I had only associated with the elderly or amputees. I couldn't believe that everything I was living through was real. I was waiting to wake up and tell myself that everything was fine and it was just a bad dream. Somehow, I believed that once I was able to sit in the wheelchair, the next step would be to get to my feet. And despite all indications otherwise, I saw hope in that objective.

On Sunday, as the time approached for me to meet with Mr Max, the entire hospital had a power failure. The generators started, but only the emergency elevator worked. Mr Max was quite old and had had hip surgery. If I understood correctly, I think he had a hip prosthesis. He walked with difficulty and climbing the stairs was certainly hard and demanding for him. But he had made it clear that he wanted to see me in a wheelchair that Sunday. So, he put the fatigue aside and came up not two or three steps or even three or four floors, but ten floors just for me! I have only known a few people like this in all my life. People dedicated to the profession and, especially, to the patient.

'I cannot believe it! Did you climb all those stairs?' I asked him when he entered the room panting.

'Did you think you could get rid of me so easily? Let's get to work. I'm going to call two nurses to carry you to the chair, so you don't get scared before we even start. Normally, I could take you alone, but since you are scared and panicky, I had to find a more comfortable option for you.'

'Thanks for being so thoughtful!' I replied laughing.

'I can take you from behind your head, one of the nurses will hold your torso and the other will hold you below the knees. I have fixed the back of the chair at seventy degrees; it may take about two to three weeks to get used to and then we will see about increasing the angle. Don't be afraid, no one will drop you. You're safe, okay? I'll put your collar on and we'll get to work.'

The three of them took me in their arms and in a few seconds, I was sitting in a wheelchair.

'How are you and how do you feel?' Mr Max asked me.

'About the same as when I am on the edge of the bed. I can't see and breathing is difficult,' I answered in a low voice.

'Close your eyes if it's easier for you and keep breathing. Someone call a nurse with a blood pressure monitor, please,' Mr Max tried to reassure me.

A nurse came and took my blood pressure. It was very low, but I kept my composure and endured the waves of nausea, and after about twenty minutes I recovered. They pushed me through the corridors of the recovery section. I also passed by Andrena so that she could see me. After about half an hour I was exhausted and I asked them to put me back into bed. I was glad I could leave my room and see things, people and different walls. Staying in bed all the time came with loneliness, which was becoming more and more unbearable. So the chair ride had been a refreshment.

'Did you like that?' Mr Max asked me after they put me to bed.

'Yes, sort of,' I answered.

'I'm going on holiday tomorrow. Mr Florin will replace me, he will take care of you. He's more direct, so listen to him and don't get upset. If you practice sitting in the wheelchair, you'll be able to go outside in front of the hospital. Mr Florin will put you in a chair and take you to the gym, where you'll practice on different machines. So work hard, okay?'

'Okay, thank you for helping me.'

Later that evening I watched TV and talked to my mother about my thoughts.

'Please ask Aunty to bring me the red bag from home where I keep my makeup when she next comes to see us.' It seemed to me that if I could manage to sit in the chair, I would soon be able to move my hands and stand up. 'I want to sit in front of the mirror and put on makeup, I want to do everything by myself. I can't wait!' I told my mother.

'Of course,' she answered, somewhat hesitantly, but I hadn't noticed. I think her soul was broken when she heard my naivety. My mother knew I would never be the same again, even though she hoped it wouldn't be that bad. She didn't have the heart to tell me, at that moment, the predictions given by the doctors, so she encouraged me to believe in the reality that everyone wanted.

'By the way, it's been a long time and August is just around the corner which means the trip to Paris with the dancers. If things haven't progressed much, and my condition is the same now, do I still have a chance of going there?'

'I don't want to make you sad, my dear, but I'm afraid you won't be able to go to Paris in August. I'm sorry. I know you really wanted to go on the trip, but we need to focus on other things.'

At first, I thought that if I could sit in the wheelchair, I would soon be able to stand up, even though at the time I couldn't even hold a glass of water to my mouth. No matter how hard I tried to control myself and how hard I fought with myself, it was as if everything had turned against me. If the first time I felt good in the wheelchair, on the second try it was like I was a different person. Mr Florin carried me by himself, because that was his working technique, but I was terribly frightened. The wheelchair had become a torment, a burden. I didn't feel safe at all. The insecurity made me panic and cry. It was even worse in the gym. He put me on an electric bicycle, which passively mobilised my lower limbs. I sat on that machine for about twenty minutes and cried the whole time. I was also doing a few exercises on a pulley with my right hand. It wasn't much, just simple movements of the forearm, but even those made me afraid. Not to mention that every time Mr Florin had to tilt the wheelchair backwards to go over door lips, I would scream for as long as my lungs held out. All the medical staff knew about my case and could hardly stand me. Most said that I was pretending and that I was too fussy and that was why I was behaving like that, not that I really had a serious problem. Most of the people I met in the physiotherapy room were old, and I was the youngest there. I felt like a person who was in the wrong place and as if I had been misdirected there.

20

I am still here

I was still sleeping badly, and when I did fall asleep, I had nightmares and cried for help. I don't know what I was dreaming about, but I found myself crying and screaming. One night, my mother was so frightened that she pressed the panic button, but the nurses had already heard my screams and come to the room. When I opened my eyes, I had no idea what had happened and why everyone had gathered around me. One possibility for my bad dreams might have been the psychiatric hospital next door. Every night I left the window open so I could feel the pleasant summer air. Every night I could hear the cries of the mentally ill accompanied by the sirens of ambulances arriving with new cases. There were always shouts, "Police, police", I don't know why, but it always made me shiver.

A doctor who specialised in psychiatry, probably from the neighbouring hospital, came to talk to me every day. She tried to lift my spirits by telling me different stories about people who had been badly injured and finally healed. Those stories didn't help me much. She also told me a poem about a cloud. She told me to imagine the cloud entering my respiratory system and gathering all my negative energies, then to imagine that I was breathing them out and leaving only the positive ones. That didn't work either. I think what I really needed was just for someone to listen to me and understand me. Maybe I was selfish, but I didn't care about other cases, I didn't even find myself in them. The psychiatrist gave me a few drops of tincture in water to calm me down. Soon, she gave up.

'If you don't want to process your situation and stop crying, you will just stay upset!' the psychiatrist growled, then she left the living room, slamming the door. That was the last time I saw her. She didn't come again.

Biology had attracted me from the first hours of the fifth grade and made me want, with all my being, to study medicine and become a doctor. In my opinion, behaviour like that by a psychiatrist does dishonour to the doctor's vocation, since it betrays a lack of understanding about the proper doctor-patient relationship. However, she was better than some of the others. As it happened, she left me staring at the sun, but she did it quietly and without disturbing me too much and leaving marks on my soul. I met other doctors who displayed such devastating behaviours that they are difficult to describe. I was most struck by Dr H., whom Professor Onose asked to take over my case.

On one critical night, around two a.m., my fever and nausea struck again. What could we do besides call the doctor on duty? My father was with me that night, and he was visibly alarmed by my condition and went down the hall and asked a nurse for help. After about fifteen minutes, Dr H. also appeared in the room, with the face of someone recently woken from sleep and carrying a can of Coke in her hand.

'Doctor, what can we do? Andreea has a high fever again and she is not feeling well,' said my father to the doctor.

'Yes, she has. Go to the pharmacy and buy her a Perfalgan,' she replied in a whiny tone, or maybe I'm wrong but honestly that's how she usually was.

What a night that was. They took blood for tests, and when they tried to give me the Perfalgan intravenously, they couldn't find an IV stand so they moved the bed next to the wall, which had a nail they could tie the bag to. Usually, the nurses would hang the IV bag on the bed, but now that the butterfly needle was fitted in my leg the tube would not reach the length of my bed.

I wasn't bothered so much by her behaviour that night, but there were other situations where her attitude was not good. She was the only doctor I met in six years with such an attitude. I do not dispute her knowledge and the fact that she studied for many years to become a doctor, but she had no empathy for the patient. In her medical practice there was no doctor-patient relationship. It was almost as if someone had pushed her into medicine. As I see things, a real and complete doctor is one who cares about the humanity of the patient.

Another situation in which Dr H. proved how "good" she was, especially as a human being, was when some reporters from Antena 1 TV came to interview me for a short fundraising appeal. I had done an interview before Professor Onose left to attend his conference, and he had allowed the reporters to enter my room. Now I needed Dr H. to allow the reporters into my room. I needed a lot of money for medicines and medical supplies, and Ramona, my cousin, had found several recovery clinics abroad, but the cost was so high, tens of thousands of euros. The people from Antena 1 had come up with the idea that I could be part of the "I Want to Help" campaign run by the Always Near Foundation, which is why I needed to do the interview. Dr H. did not agree and so my mother had to go outside in front of the hospital to be interviewed there, without me. After the interview, she asked my mother what we wanted to do with the money from the campaign and if we wanted to buy a house or go to visit relatives from abroad. Well, God forgive me if I'm wrong about this, but such a person has absolutely no place in the medical profession. At this point I had been in a bed for three months, and my parents were struggling all the time, and you, the doctor, come and ask us if we're asking for money so we can go abroad on holiday to visit relatives? What heart do you have and how can you call yourself a doctor with such an attitude?

In my opinion, the doctor is that dedicated and involved person, who first-and-foremost, after God, has the ability to save lives. We know that the doctor is also a human being, and this means having good, but also less good, emotions. Doctors experience fears, anxieties, tiredness and exhaustion. Despite this, the doctor is curious, constantly evolving, responsible, empathetic, patient, and always aware of what they are doing. Medicine is not just about theory and the love of science; it is primarily about people. You go into medicine because you love people, you love to help them, and you love the way they are and function. Medicine sits at the point between science and consciousness, and this means that the doctor can combine the two elements to overcome harsh diagnoses and death. The doctor puts their training into practice, using the right tools to treat and cure the suffering of the person next to him or her. The doctor knows that beyond treatments and medical devices, there is concern and interest in the human being. And Hippocrates knew this when he said that "Where the art of medicine is loved, there is also a love for humanity."

21

Just say sorry

Meanwhile, one afternoon, in Bacău, my aunt (my father's brother's wife), returned from work to find an older woman and a young man waiting for her in front of her block.

'Hello. I'm Alex's grandmother – the boy who caused the accident. Please, I would like to talk and to help,' said the woman.

'Hello. I don't think we have anything to talk about,' replied my aunt.

'Ma'am, it's about our children. Nobody wanted this to happen.'

'You confuse me. I'm Andreea's aunt, not her mother.' (My aunt and mother have the same name, hence the confusion. The woman probably searched the directory for our address and the first one she found was my aunt's.)

'I'm sorry about what happened. Tell me where the girl is now, we would like to visit her.'

'I understand, the situation is quite serious, I would not like to be in your shoes, but even less in the place of her parents. They are in Bucharest, Andreea is in hospital there.'

'I want to talk to her parents, please.'

'Leave me your number and I'll talk to my brother-in-law; if he agrees, I'll call you to give you his phone number.'

When someone hurts us, willingly or unwillingly, we humans tend to shy away from those people or even reject them. At least for a while. This is because we need time. Time to get used to what has happened. Time to understand how and why we were put in such extreme situations. But the one who made a mistake and really wants to help or apologise has a duty to do everything possible to be seen and understood by the person who they hurt. If they give up on the first try, I tend to think their intention wasn't real. After a while, my father talked to Alex's grandmother. I can't remember the discussion in detail, but it went something like – "I go to church to pray that the girl will recover". I mean, they wanted to help, but they didn't do anything concrete. In six years, I personally have not even received an "I'm sorry" from him. I don't know what sort of conscience you must have to have to deal with such a situation with such indifference, but it seems to me to be an attitude lacking in any trace of humanity. Anyway, who am I to judge? Sooner or later we all pay in one form or another for our actions.

22

Help me by listening

In the last two weeks of June, everything seemed to go crazy. No one and nothing pleased me. Dad had exhausted all possible forms of days off work, so he had to return to Bacău to work. He worked twenty-four hour shifts with three-day breaks so he could return to me. In order to help my mother while my father was working my family looked for a woman to help with me. They found Mihaela, a lady in her fifties, but she didn't last long around me. I admit that I was very difficult, and it must have been tough to put up with me because no one could really understand, better than me, what I felt physically and mentally.

Around that time, I met a young man in his thirties, Marius, who had befriended Andrena, the young woman who had been hospitalised after the car accident where her boyfriend had died. Andrena had good intentions. She wanted to introduce him to me to raise my spirits and so that I could spend time with other people. He had had a motorcycle accident and had also suffered a spinal cord injury, but he had been less affected than me. He couldn't use his lower limbs at all, but his torso and upper limbs were fine. He could feed and dress himself, move to one side, even drive an adapted car, so he could do many more things than I could do. When we met, he came across as somebody who thought he knew everything. How could he raise my morale when his behaviour made me sad and instead of encouraging me, he made me cry and hate my situation even more?

'You are too spoiled. Your parents should go and leave you alone, then you will be able to see how hard your situation could be. You do nothing but cry and torment those around you. I was confined to bed after the accident, but I didn't complain and look, I'm very independent today, even if I'm in a wheelchair,' he told me.

'Please go, leave. Get out. I can't stand you; I hate you, get out,' I replied, screaming and bursting into tears.

It's hard for me to understand people like that. People who believe that because they have faced hardship, they are superior to others. People who try to show others that if they have passed a test others should be like them, without weighing up the situation the other person is going through. I agree that everyone can be a good example and inspiration to their neighbour, but they cannot do it by humiliating and shaming the person in question, as Marius did with me. We humans are unique. We live and react to experiences differently. Some need more time to overcome trauma, others less. Some people are more solid and manage to rebalance themselves even after experiencing extreme suffering which marks their existence. Others remain anchored in that pain all their lives and give up looking for solutions for a better life. We can all contribute to other people's well-being, but not by criticising and telling them that they are not doing anything to help themselves. It does not help a person if you give examples of people who have managed to overcome similar situations because everyone has their own rhythm. Instead, you help the person if you listen to them, see what is troubling them and support them. You help a person if you make them feel that their existence is important. You help the individual by entering and staying in their life, by sitting with them and giving them moments that bring a smile to their face.

Some more tough days passed, and I was very close to losing my mind. I couldn't bear to see the light of day anymore and I made my family draw the curtains over the window. The pills I was given by the psychiatrist before I was taken to the infectious disease hospital probably had a negative effect on me. I started saying things I didn't want to say, not in delirium, but things would come out of my mouth that I didn't really want to say. I started to yell at my parents, I told them I hated them and to leave me alone, then when I realised what I was saying, I apologised and explained to them what was happening to me, that I didn't mean to behave like that.

I felt like no one understood me anymore, and my parents, afraid of upsetting me, stopped talking to me. I was on a constant perfusion, being pumped full of different supplements that were supposed to give me more strength. Those pills also cost lots of money. In addition to those, I had other treatments administered through the butterfly needle. So many fluids went through my veins that once about four nurses took turns trying to insert a new needle, without success. When they saw that it was failing, they wanted to put a catheter in my neck. It was the first medical intervention that I completely rejected. My face and neck were the only parts of my body I felt when someone touched me. On the right side of my neck are the scars of spinal surgery, and now they wanted to inscribe the other side using a catheter. I objected, begging the nurses not to put my catheter in because I was no longer able to bear the idea and the pain. Eventually they understood and talked to Professor Onose, who had just returned from the conference. They made the decision to leave me without a needle for two days and give me oral treatments instead of the intravenous ones. On the third day, they succeeded in fitting a butterfly needle.

I don't know how a person feels in life's last seconds, but I would associate those moments with a shudder. A cold shiver in the throat, nose and whole body, as if all the organs were freezing. A shudder which I felt for two nights when the border of the world beyond was very close to me. Two nights in which, without being aware and remembering, I horrified my mother, telling her that I was going to die because that was how it was conveyed to me. I think my soul was on the verge of being among the angels; however, God wanted me to stay here on earth; he was testing me in what felt like an experiment, and putting me through very hard times.

23

Stubborn and strong

While I was in Bagdasar, the nurses helped my mother to wash my hair on the edge of the bed. They would lie me across the bed, put my feet on a chair so that they wouldn't dangle on the floor, and a nurse would hold my torso on the edge. They put water in buckets, which they brought to the bed. One nurse held my head, another washed my hair with shampoo and my mother poured water on my hair, which was caught in the bowl.

'Hey girl, the back of your hair is tangled, worse than last time! It's like wool, what should we do?' asked Kitten, one of the nurses, whose name I didn't know, but everyone called Kitten.

'I don't know, but a haircut is not an option!' I answered.

'Let me dry her hair and then I will call you to turn her on one side and I'll try to untangle the back of her hair,' my mother said.

My mother tried to comb my hair, but she couldn't manage much with the tangles. She struggled for a few hours, then I stopped her because I couldn't take it anymore. She also bought me some hair conditioner, but because I was always lying in bed, there wasn't anything to prevent my hair from becoming tangled and matted. I couldn't sit in the wheelchair for long, and even if I did, she still couldn't comb my hair because I couldn't hold my head up, and the back of the chair was very high.

In all, June left a deep mark on me. This was not helped by a new resident doctor who had little empathy and behaved very harshly with me. I was still in the habit of spitting out the secretions that gathered in my throat, as I was still afraid of being aspirated, like they did in the ICU unit, and this doctor was disturbed by my gesture. She told me that it was not justified that I was still spitting, and she refused to let my mother give me a napkin.

'Why are you crying now?' the doctor asked me. I don't know her name, but I still remember her face.

'I can't keep my saliva in my mouth anymore, I want to spit!' I answered.

'No way. I explained to you that there is no reason for you to spit. Swallow it or I will spit on you.'

My despair was reaching alarming heights. I spat on myself, because I couldn't breathe and hold all my saliva in my mouth at the same time. That woman, who also held the title of resident physician, had humiliated me entirely. Reader, if you choose to go into medicine for the money or because you feel forced into it, you would do better to stay at home. Stop destroying people's souls. Don't come and work in a field where you are not suited, there's no point. You are destroying your life and the lives of others. The conflict with the doctor must have reached Dr H.'s ears – not my intention – because she stopped checking on me.

Luckily, besides all the negative examples in that hospital, which, unfortunately, were many, there were also dedicated doctors, led by Professor Onose. I met one very nice resident doctor, who made me smile.

'Can I drink fizzy juice or at least fizzy water and eat a small bag of chips?' I asked the resident one morning.

'Hmm, okay. You can drink fizzy juice and eat a bag of chips, but don't overdo it, okay? And be sure to eat something that is also healthy, as I told you.'

'Super, thank you very much. I will also eat something healthy, but I will not get close to the chicken liver. I'm sorry but I cannot.'

Among other things, my albumin was very low, and every time Dr D. came to see me, she encouraged me to eat liver so as to increase my albumin levels. As a child, I was quite picky about food, and after a negative experience in kindergarten, with a teacher who forced me to eat even what I didn't like, I became even more selective and picky about food, and the liver was one of many foods I couldn't get even close to.

'Please tell me you ate liver,' Dr D. asked me one afternoon when she was on duty.

'No, and I can't. Please understand me, I really don't like it,' I answered.

'But you have to understand that your albumin must increase, and if you don't eat liver, it won't happen. At least a piece or two. I'll bring it in, and we'll eat it together.'

'No, no, no! Can't you give me some liver replacement pills?'

'Not really...'

'That is a shame, because I don't eat liver.'

'Oh, but you're so stubborn. What is your star sign?'

'Leo.'

'Aha, then of course! Stubborn and strong.'

'Yes ... how long will it take for me to recover? When can I start walking again?'

'I don't know, you have to be patient!'

'Well, what do the medical books say?'

'Well ... recovery can take between six months and two years.'

'Two years; does that mean I have to stay in hospital for two years?'

'Not quite, not exactly. If your condition improves – if you eat liver,' she said with a laugh, 'and things go well, you will be able to go home.'

'Will I go home like this? Without being able to move at all. How can I be at home like that? I must stay in the hospital until I'm well, I can't go home like this.'

'Let time decide and be patient. I'm going to see a few more patients. I'm on duty. In case you change your mind – let me know so we can order liver and eat it together,' she told me, giving me a big smile.

After Dr D. left, I stayed with Mihaela, because my father had to go to Bacău, to work, and my mother went to Piata Sudului to buy me some things, including fruit jellies. In addition to the many pills I took, I had some very bitter syrups to swallow, so the jellies were welcome. Meanwhile, Andrena came to my room with her mother.

'Have you eaten anything today, girl?' Andrena asked me. She was from Craiova, and her accent was very nice.

'Mhh, yes, some watermelon. Would you like some?'

'Have you only eaten only watermelon until now – four in the afternoon?'

'Yes, I have to admit.'

'Do you want to get out of the hospital this year?'

'I want to, but Dr D. told me that recovery can take two years.'

'And you listened to her? These doctors say all sorts of things. Let's call some nurses to put you in the wheelchair and get you out, let's go for a walk. Okay?'

'How can I go out like this? With a needle in my arm and with my shitty face?'

'Come on, girl, it doesn't matter. Do you know how many of us gather in front of the hospital every night? With needles, without, with crutches, wheelchairs, everything, the important thing is that we feel good.'

'Don't be upset, but I don't want to. You should know that I don't feel comfortable in my wheelchair and I'm afraid of crossing the thresholds, and there are a lot of thresholds in front of the hospital. At the doors, by the elevator, everywhere! And the ramp in front of the hospital, which is very long and steep. I remember when they brought me in with the stretcher how steep the ramp is. I felt like I would fall over my head on the stretcher, as if I was climbing a mountain. If I felt like that with the stretcher, do you realise how it would feel in the wheelchair?'

Andrena really wanted to help me, I always liked her attitude and her positivity. However, my adaptation to the situation I was going through was quite slow.

24

My mother's pain

Another situation that left a deep impression on me was when the plastic surgeon, who had operated on my left hand, took off the bandage and showed me the result.

'Mum, this is not my hand! Where's my hand? What happened to it?' I asked my mother, almost crying.

'It will need more operations to make it look better, don't be sad.'

The two fingers in the middle were deformed and covered in scars, and the skin did not even look like skin. The parts of my hand where my skin had been ripped off during the accident were replaced with the skin from my left thigh – it looked disgusting. My hand was dirty, covered in murky stuff from all the solutions and creams they put on as treatment, and that made it look even more sinister. Later in the afternoon, when I was lying on my side and had managed to fall asleep, my mother started to try and clean my hand. It took her about three days before she managed to completely clean my hand.

The last days of June and, in the event, the last days I spent at Bagdasar Hospital, almost knocked me down. They moved me to another room, much smaller than the special room I had been staying in. A room with a single bed, an armchair and a shared bathroom. In doing this, they sentenced my mother to even more torment. As it was she only managed to get a few hours of sleep because she had to take care of me day and night, and trying to sleep in an armchair, when she could rest, really finished her off. She could not rest at all. Her feet swelled enormously from all the standing, and now she could hardly stand on them. I had never seen her mad in the three months since the accident, but I could see how much suffering and stress she was accumulating. One day, for the first time, she lost her temper. She told me that she could no longer bear any of what was happening and that she would not be sorry if she died. I did not get upset. I understood her. She's human after all and she had to unload somehow. It is not easy to stay in hospitals for three months, with the situation you are going through getting worse instead of improving.

They moved me out of that special room because normally you would have to pay one hundred euros a day to be able to stay there. My parents didn't have the money and made several requests to the hospital management, so I managed to stay there for a while. Eventually, a patient came who wanted to stay there and had money, so they moved me, regardless of the circumstances. That man was on his feet, but he had some back problems, and because he was in a very good financial situation, he took the room for the comfort. I just wanted peace and understanding, I had learnt from previous experience that I did not enjoy staying in large wards with many patients. But because money always comes first, they pushed me aside and moved me to that little room.

'Hey Kitten, how's the room?' Professor Onose asked me during the visit.

'It's hard, very hard. Mum can't cope anymore,' I answered.

'I can imagine, but it was the only solution. In a few days you will leave for the Nicolae Robănescu Children's Recovery Hospital, where Dr Pădure is waiting for you. I've been consulting with her since you've been with us. You will like it there, it is much more beautiful, you will meet other children your age. It will be good, you will see.'

Over the next few days, my situation got worse again. The fever returned and I was taken to several wards for investigation. My habit of spitting up secretions had almost disappeared, I rarely did it more than a few times a day – however, it was replaced with a few days of spitting blood clots. Due to the fever, I couldn't do any physical therapy. So my small progress there came to a halt as well. Two nights before leaving for the new hospital, Andrena came to say goodbye because she was going home. She came walking, leaning on a frame. She still had to fight, but the fact that she had regained her independence and that she could take steps meant a lot. I was very happy for her, but also saddened, thinking that she, three months after her accident, was standing, whereas I was not even able to hold my head up or bring my hand to my face.

'Mom, when will I be like Andrena?'

'I hope it happens soon, my dear.'

25

Fighting for life

On 1st July, at noon, they took me to Robănescu Hospital. It was very hot outside. It was not too far between the two hospitals, and it didn't take us long to get there. Nonetheless, I was filled with panic, fearing that we would have an accident, and I cried all the way. They took me out of the ambulance and carried me up a ramp as steep as the one at Bagdasar. I waited in the hall until Dr Padure came.

'Dad, where have you brought me? Is it a church?' I asked. Lying on the stretcher, immobilised, I could see only the huge ceiling of the hall, which was connected to the upper floor, and there were dozens of icons.

'Trust me, stay calm, it will be fine.'

The head nurse in the recovery department of Bagdasar Hospital had made a colossal mistake, which now affected me hugely. In the documents, instead of transferring me to the recovery hospital, she discharged me, and according to the rules, you cannot have a discharge and a hospitalisation on the same day. Thus, after tens of minutes of waiting, in which solutions were sought for me, and none were found, I had to return to Bagdasar, and stay there another day only to return to the recovery hospital the following day! I had a fever and was sick, but there was nothing I could do. My father had to return to Bacău in the evening, so we obtained an agreement and were allowed to leave most of our luggage at the new hospital, so that my mother would not have to struggle by herself the next day, and we returned to Bagdasar. Basically, I was no longer an in-patient anywhere, I was on my own, but the people from Bagdasar had to receive me back because it was their fault. But if something had happened, no one would have been held accountable, except maybe the head nurse for completing the papers incorrectly.

We returned to the recovery hospital the next day. They took me to one of the ICU units, where I stayed for another three weeks. The nurses and infirmieres spent about two hours taking care of me. They took my biological samples and removed my urinary catheter, choosing intermittent catheterisation every five to six hours instead of the permanent one. I was in a larger room with three beds. Even in intensive care, there are differences between a regular and a paediatric hospital – there were spots of colour on the white walls.

There was another boy in the room, Aryan, who was about ten years old. His parents were with him. What I saw made me very sad. Aryan didn't look like an ordinary child. He was very thin, barely fifteen kilograms. He wasn't talking. Nor moving. He did not take his parents in his arms. He didn't play. He didn't do anything that a child his age usually does, he just growled and cried sometimes. His parents carried him in their arms. He couldn't even drink water. He had a nasogastric tube in his nose, into which his parents fed him mashed food. They also gave him his medication through that tube. They aspirated him daily, as I had been aspirated in ICU. They even aspirated him for two to three hours a day, and he did not react at all. He didn't refuse anything. I watched those scenes in terror, knowing how awful that feeling was, and I wondered how he could stand it without having a reaction. I later realised that he had a serious condition that had affected his brain. However, I could not imagine how such a thing could exist. How can a child suffer so much and not know how beautiful life is?

At that hospital, I met hundreds of children like Aryan. Children who were practically unaware of reality. Children who were just breathing. They just existed. They had no idea what was going on around them. Many of them were born with various disorders and would never know what it was like to lead a normal life. Next to them were destroyed parents. Parents who fought for the existence of children from their first minutes of life. Parents who had given up their personal lives and had been in hospitals for years, hoping for progress. Some were making progress; others were the same after fifteen years. It was even worse to see broken relationships and marriages when the troubles of the children had badly affected the lives of the parents. There were also several wards in the hospital with abandoned children who had been deserted by their parents after the onset of the disease. I felt like I had lived in another world before the accident. The world I knew was full of joys, beautiful moments and moments of happiness.

I liked the whole team at the hospital. They were all dedicated and involved in what they were doing. Dr Pădure, the hospital manager and the doctor in charge of my case, gave me another of life's lessons. At first, she seemed a bit harsh, then, when I got to know her better, I discovered what a beautiful person she was. She was born prematurely and was left with a small physical defect. On her upper limbs, she doesn't have all her fingers, only five out of ten, but that hasn't stopped her. The precision with which she injects the patient's muscle is extraordinary. At the first visit, my mother was sad and with tears in her eyes.

'Why do you put on this face? You must improve on that. You are not helping Andreea like this,' the doctor told my mother.

'I have no other face!' my mother replied.

So much was burdening my mother, and the suffering was showing on her face. My mother has always been a person who, when she has a problem, reveals it. She couldn't hold anything back that bothered her. On the other hand, the doctor spoke from experience. For someone who is going through a serious situation, it is overwhelming to see those around them suffering. It is perfectly normal for parents to cry and suffer because of the child's pain, but they should control showing their emotions, otherwise the confidence and security that they transfer to their child decreases. That's why the doctor tried to warn my mother.

26

Baby steps

For the first week, at the new hospital I did physiotherapy in my room. The physiotherapists, Adrian and Iulian, came daily to mobilise my limbs at bed level. Oh, how patient they were with me and how much the two of them endured me! In theory, they should have put me in a wheelchair and taken me to the physiotherapy room, but as I became very agitated when someone moved me, they gave me a week to acclimatise in my own room.

In addition to physical therapy, I did occupational therapy and psychotherapy. For the occupational therapy, two very nice ladies came to the room, Ani and Mari, to passively mobilise my fingers. At psychotherapy, things were not as good. Mrs psychologist V. told me different stories about animals and kept insisting that I go to her office. I was not at all happy with the proposal and I did not understand why she insisted upon it. She demanded more than the physiotherapists did. For physical therapy I understood the importance of going to the gym. There were special worktables and much more, but the psychotherapy was the same in whichever room it happened in. I had expected her to understand me more and be patient with me.

I started going to the gym, with Mr Adi, the physiotherapist. Fear totally paralysed me, and I cried a lot. In the gym, the physiotherapists used a different technique to transfer me from the wheelchair and I needed time to get used to it. The therapist gripped me under my armpits, and someone else held my knees, or there was another option with the sheet, but I didn't like that at all, so they didn't use it. The technique was safe, but I could not control myself and my fear because of the lack of control over my body. Mr Iulian, my second physiotherapist, went on vacation and left Bogdan to take care of me and take me to the gym. Bogdan was younger than the other two and tried every way to convince me to come to the gym voluntarily. He failed to convince me. I couldn't stop crying and screaming, I annoyed him a lot, but he still took me to the gym. It was the only time in six years that I saw him so irritated.

The gym was not easy to get to. There were thresholds to cross, even at the elevator, and when I entered the room and saw what a high table I had to sit on, I was even more terrified. The height of the table was no more than a meter, but I perceived it as five meters high. Seen from the outside, the room was very nicely decorated, with mirrors, lots of cherry and blue physiotherapy tables and lots of appliances. Next to the cherry table where I was placed there was a large aquarium with orange fish. That room was just one of many, at least twenty, I think. Although it looked nice, from the inside, the room was full of pain. Full of children like Aryan. However, there were also some stories that gave you a glimmer of hope.

'Cute fishes! I also had fishes at home, up until last year, when Mustăcilă died, but it had lived for about two years.' I told Bogdan while he was mobilizing my limbs.

'Well you see, girl? I told you I was bringing you to a beautiful place and instead of being happy, you yelled at me,' he replied.

'I'll try not to yell tomorrow, but I can't promise!'

'Don't make me sad! Do you want to argue every day? I don't understand, why are you scared? Have you ever been dropped on the ground?'

'No, I'm just scared because I can't help myself and I don't feel safe when someone moves me.'

'We are strong, we won't drop you. You have to trust us. Do you do the same to Adi? Iulian told me that you didn't agree before he went on holiday.'

'I seem to trust Mr Adi more, I don't cry as much with him. It's just that he's better made – stronger than you.'

'What do you mean?'

'You are weaker, smaller, I thought you would not have the strength to lift me.'

'And now it is clear to you that you are safe?'

'Not really...'

I gave a little, and so did he, and somehow, we reached an agreement. In the following days I continued to cry but then we became friends. Anyway, all the staff in the hospital supported and understood me, except the psychologist, Mrs V. In the end, I went to her office. I don't know how she did it, but she made me cry and hate myself even more. At the last meeting I couldn't stand it anymore and I broke out.

'Don't be upset, but all these questions seem useless to me,' I told her after she had asked me again what kind of bird and what kind of flower I would be.

'Why do you think this?'

'Because these questions annoy me and don't help me at all. You would do better asking me about me. You would do better telling me something to help me get through these days.'

'Did you apologise to your parents?'

'For what?'

'For what you did!'

'Is that how you think you're helping me? Call my father now! I want to go!' I cried.

'You are like a hedgehog. No one will help you if you do not change your behaviour.'

'I hate you! I can't stand you anymore!'

'Look, see? You're just like a hedgehog!'

'I don't want to see or talk to you again; I can't stand you. Dad, get me out of here, please.'

'Okay, another colleague of mine will pick you up. It is clear that we do not understand each other, but I repeat, if you do not review your behaviour, you will not get well.'

27

Looking for good

I had some difficult days in that hospital too. Days with high fever
and a lot of pain. The fever was caused by a severe urinary tract
infection that did not want to leave me. The infection was a result
of the long-term catheters I had before I arrived at the recovery
hospital. I was now maintained by intermittent catheterisation.
The change of hospital was hard for my parents, especially my
mother, who was with me night and day. The routine was different
from Bagdasar. No one came to turn me or to wash me in the
mornings, as they had in the hospital for infectious diseases. My
mother had to adapt and do almost everything on her own. My
father helped her when he was not at work; otherwise my mother
had to ask an infirmiere to help. Remembering how the nurses in
Bagdasar handled me, my mother had to do everything they did.
She learnt to turn me with the sheet, to dress me, to wash me. The
nurses even taught my mother how to drain my catheter every five
to six hours. It was not easy for me to get used to all this. It was
not easy for me mentally to accept that someone else had to take
care of me. It's not easy to know that in a few weeks you will be
fourteen years old, and you will have been in hospitals for almost
four months and be totally dependent on others, wearing nappies,
with someone else having to wipe your ass because you can't
control your intestines.

I started talking less and I was no longer smiling or eating much. The doctors called the psychiatrist who had given me some medicine two months ago, which should have made me feel better and made me smile. The psychiatrist was the wife of a doctor from the hospital, so she arrived pretty quickly. When I returned from physiotherapy, I found her in the room, sitting on a pink chair.

'Hello, Andreea! How are you? How are you feeling?' she asked.

'Just like I was when you last saw me.'

'I see progress. Last time you were in bed, now you can sit in a wheelchair.'

'Yes, but I still can't move.'

'You have to trust yourself and not lose hope! I came to increase your dose a little of the treatment I gave you. I hope it will make you feel better, and smile more.'

It wasn't like that. The pills didn't make me smile. They fooled me and made things worse. They made me drowsy. After the gym at one p.m., I slept until about seven p.m. Then, at night, I would stare at the walls. I wasn't good for anything anymore.

I allowed my mother to turn me once during the day at noon and twice at night, once at eleven p.m. and once again at three a.m.; the rest of the time I was on my back face up. My bed was by the window and I enjoyed what I saw in the nearby building. There were always two cats sitting at one of the windows of the building. The sight of them made me happy. I have always loved cats. I used to bring cats I found on the street to the garden in front of the balcony at home or put them in the cellar. I made them cribs and fed them. The cats in the neighbourhood knew where to find food, and because our flat was on the ground floor, they would jump in through the balcony window during the summer. My mother had lots of flower pots on the balcony, and every time a cat jumped in the balcony, it left footprints and broken flower pots.

'I like cats too. I have Mițiloanca in the occupational therapy room. If you come to therapy, you can see her,' said Ani, the occupational therapist, who had come to the salon to mobilise my fingers.

'Cool! I will come, but not now. The ramp at the entrance to your office is too steep,' I replied.

'I understand, it's okay. You will overcome this fear as well. When you are ready, Miți is waiting for you there. Until then I will come to you.'

Because I went out of the ward every day to go to different therapies, I met several children who were in the hospital. I knew the story of Ivana, a little girl of about ten or eleven years old, who was in the other ICU ward. She was also in the hospital due to a car accident. She also suffered a spinal cord injury, but at a lower level than mine and so she could use her upper body. Her grandmother or aunt took care of her, I'm not sure which, but I think it was the aunt. Ivana was not the only victim in the car accident she suffered. Her mother and sister died instantly, and her father was injured and is in hospital. It's hard to imagine all this, let alone live it. Her aunt used to talk to my mother and sometimes she would come to us in the room. I saw her crying many times.

I also learnt Vali's story, a boy the same age as me, who had been paralysed from the waist down due to an injection. Mrs Mioara, his mother, looked after him. I liked their attitude, they were always in a good mood. Vali went through very hard times. By the time he reached the recovery hospital, he had lost a lot of weight and the doctors who had given him the wrong injection had not treated him properly. When I met him, he had a deep pressure sore, a wound in the sacral area. It was as large as a plate. All the flesh was gone and the bone was visible. His mother struggled to look after him, but in the end they came out victorious. He was lucky, and in about two or three years he fully recovered.

28

Just the person I needed

My hair was getting so tangled my mother could barely comb it. There was a hairdresser near the hospital and my mother bought a hair net, hoping that she might use it to save my hair. Mrs Vali, the dearest and most attached to me, helped my mother wash my hair on the edge of the bed.

The scar on my neck, from the operation, was starting to heal and they had to wash that area too, because there were traces of the bandage left. But it was sensitive and washing it aggravated me. Against my will, my mother and Mrs Vali tried to give my neck a little wash, and I started to shake and tremble. As I jiggled, the little untangled hair that I had left got knotted too. The hair net had no effect, and all my hair matted into a large lump. Chunks of my hair had fallen out due to the stress of the last months, so I already had a few bald patches.

The next day, my mother asked a hairdresser to come to the hospital to see if she could do something to my hair. Unfortunately, nothing could be done.

'Honey, I'm sorry, but I have to cut your hair at the back. There's nothing else I can do, it's like wool,' the hairdresser told me.

'Okay ...' I replied resignedly, thinking that in the last few months my opinion had ceased to matter anyway; I just had to swallow it, whether I liked it or not.

'I will also cut your remaining hair, so that I can give it a bit of shape.'

I had very long hair, down to my buttocks, and I cared a lot about it, but I had to agree to say goodbye to it. Now, I was bald at the back, and I had a little hair in front, just enough to show that I was a girl. With the remaining hair, the hairdresser made me a braided ponytail, so that it wouldn't get tangled for a while. I looked in the mirror and didn't recognise myself anymore. I looked like the ugliest girl in the world. I didn't look like Andreea at all, the girl I knew four months ago. My soul was burning, but I didn't have the strength to express myself.

On the same day, after returning from Mr Adi, I met Mrs Laura, the psychologist I was referred to by Mrs V. Mrs Laura was an extremely beautiful person, inside and out. She is a lady who will remain in my soul forever. I was exhausted at the time. I no longer had the disposition to have a dialogue.

'Don't be upset, but I don't feel like talking today, I'm not feeling well,' I told Mrs Laura.

'That's fine! I'll come back tomorrow to see how you are, and when you are ready you can come to my office,' she answered in a lovely voice.

I was pleasantly surprised by Mrs Laura's attitude, by the fact that she understood me and did not insist at all, compared to Mrs V. Over the following days we became friends, and she began to be very dear to me. I liked her from the first sessions we had together. She didn't force me to say more than I wanted to. At first, I cried a lot, but I didn't cry because of her, I cried because I had different emotions about what I was going through. She didn't force me to stay with her longer than I wanted. If I only wanted to stay ten minutes, she wouldn't insist and wouldn't try to persuade me to stay. She never bored me with therapeutic stories, I was always just talking about myself. Sometimes she would tell me about herself. She really was the right person in the right place, just the person I needed.

The evenings were always very long, especially those when my butterfly needle got clogged and it took about an hour to get one into another vein. Even more exciting were the evenings when, after fixing a new needle and delivering about half a bag of the perfusion, it would clog up again. The strongest antibiotics were circulating in my veins. Eventually, those antibiotics paid off, my fever dropped, and I felt better somehow. Also in the evening, before going to bed, after taking the oral medication, which always made me feel sick, a nurse would come to help my mother arrange my pillow.

'Please make it fluffy,' I asked Mrs Doiniţa. The pillow was very hard and if it wasn't shaken or "puffed up" the cotton wool would not sit inside it properly and my head would hurt. That's why every night someone "puffed" my pillow.

'Sure, my dear! I'll try to puff it as well as I can,' she replied.

After the sorting out of the pillow, there was an oppressive silence. Aryan had been discharged and I was left alone with my mother in the room. I didn't have a TV or anything to listen to. I had difficulties falling asleep and then at three a.m., I was turned onto another side and after that I rarely fell back asleep. I spent most of the nights looking out of the window, waiting for the morning light. Thanks to those two nights without someone sharing the hospital room my mother was able to lie down in the spare bed. Normally, she slept on the floor, on a mobile mattress, which gave her serious back pain.

29

You're going home

'I have good news,' my father told me on Monday morning.

'Surprise me!' I answered.

'On Friday, we are going home.'

'God forbid.'

'Why does this make you unhappy?'

'I don't want to go home. How can I go home like this, in this state? I don't want to go home until I get better and start walking.'

In all I hadn't recovered nearly as much as I had hoped. I could move my right upper arm and forearm, but these movements didn't help me at all. With my left arm I could sketch a few gestures from my shoulder and elbow, but this was also useless. I couldn't feed myself; I couldn't do anything with this so-called progress. The rest of my body was inert.

'It's your birthday soon and the other day you said you wanted to celebrate your birthday at home.'

'What is there to celebrate and how can I do it? Lying in a bed? Besides, I don't have the same set up and facilities at home.'

'Ramo has taken care of this, she has ordered you a special bed, like the one from Bagdasar hospital, with a remote control and everything you need. She also ordered some special pillows to sleep on, but also other things that will be useful. We will stay at home for one month at most, then return to the hospital for recovery. We will look for other clinics and maybe even go to a clinic in Germany.'

'But what if I'm sick or have a fever?'

'Let's hope this doesn't happen, stop thinking about negative things. Everyone is waiting for you at home.'

'They want to see me as I was before, not like this.'

The reason for this sudden change was that hospitalisation in a recovery hospital funded by the Romanian state had several rules. One of those rules says that a patient cannot be hospitalised for more than three consecutive weeks, regardless of their condition, because they cannot reimburse the health centre for expenses for a longer period than three weeks. Basically, it doesn't matter if you die or live, the Romanian state sends you home to be taken care of by whoever can, and if no one can, God have mercy on you.

I did not receive the news of my return home well; I was not at all happy. I kept thinking about the days ahead. In the hospital, good or bad, I was still talking to different people, I was seeing people, but at home what would I do, what would I see? The thought of loneliness pressed in on me the most.

'Well, sweetheart, you're going home on Friday, aren't you?' Mrs Mioara, Vali's mother, asked me.

'Yeah ...' I sighed.

'Wow, what a joy. We're leaving on Friday too, Vali's been so happy since we got the news. But what about you, aren't you happy?'

'Not really...'

'How can you not be happy? You will meet your friends, you will be with your relatives, how can this not be a reason for joy?'

'Yeah, I hope it's as you say!'

'Surely it will! But until Friday, I say, let's live in the moment! Let's go outside, you promised to come out with us, at least in front of the hospital. Vali is coming, so are your parents. It's so warm and nice outside!'

'I am not in the mood...'

'Come on, Andreea, it will do you good!'

'Yes, baby, let's all go out!' my father agreed.

'Pff, fine, but I can't stay long and before we go, please could you dress me in something more beautiful?'

'Sure, my love, we will dress you in whatever you want. I'll take all the clothes out of the closet, and you tell me what you choose,' my mother replied.

I chose a black T-shirt which had nice writing on it, and a pair of blue three-quarter-length trousers. After my parents had dressed me, my father put on my cervical collar and pulled the chair next to the bed, then he grabbed me by the arms, and my mother below my knees, and they put me in the chair.

'Sit me in front of the mirror, leave me for two minutes and then we can leave,' I told my father.

I was terrified at the thought of seeing myself again, but I still felt the need to look in the mirror. I had lost a lot of weight, the features of my face had changed, the bald patches on my head could be seen through the little hair I had left, I was horrible. I was looking at a different person, not the me of four months ago. Oh, what a fool you are, I thought to myself. Andreea, the one you are looking for in the mirror died on 27th March, you won't find her again!

Apart from the times when I was transferred from one hospital to another, I had not been outside. I had seen the light of day during these transfers, but I could not enjoy it as it didn't even take five minutes to get me out of the hospital and into the ambulance and then I couldn't concentrate on what was around me. It was completely different now. I sat in the hospital yard for about twenty minutes. I didn't say anything. I was just looking left and right. I hadn't done that in four months. The wind was light, and it was so nice, but I felt weird. I couldn't be happy. I was tied to an object and my body was actually frozen. The thought that I had once been different saddened me and going out hurt me more. There were different scenes playing out in my mind of times when I was happy, and I felt like I was suffocating. I no longer had the strength to cry, although I would have liked to.

'I don't want to stay here anymore. Please can you take me back to the room?' I asked my parents.

I didn't even want to eat that evening. I was beginning to understand my condition and that it will be like this for a long time, like it or not. Maybe, in my situation, some would choose to end their days, I thought in the silence of my room. But I was thinking in vain, I was not even able to die.

30

Mixing memories

On Friday morning, I was woken up by the little girl in the bed next to mine crying. She was about seven years old and had been in a coma for several days. She had fainted during the end-of-year celebration at school. It was meningitis but now she was beginning to recover. She got off lightly. Although she would go through hard times, in six months she would be fully recovered.

'I can't stand that noise anymore,' I told my mother.

'I believe you, baby, in a few hours we will go home, and you will have peace,' she replied.

The girl's mother probably heard me when I said that I couldn't stand the noise anymore, and it certainly wasn't nice for her, but I didn't say it to be mean. In fact I couldn't cope with anything and couldn't stand what was happening to me. I know that everyone in that hospital had a serious problem, but it seemed like too much to me. I had them all, I had nothing left. I thought that if I had hit myself on the head, I would have been better off; at least I wouldn't have had to consciously endure all the physical and mental pain. I wouldn't have had to face reality. Maybe it would have been harder for my parents not to be able to communicate with me, but they would certainly have been calmer than they were at this moment.

My father entered with all the luggage in his hands. 'Good morning.'

'Morning, did you manage to get everything from the dormitory?' I replied.

'Yes, I think so. Were you able to rest?'

'Yes, Andreea less. Let's hope she sleeps better at home,' my mother sighed.

'Good morning. And who's going home today?' a nurse who came to do my treatment, the last one, asked me with a smile.

'I'm leaving,' I replied. 'Will you also remove my butterfly needle after treatment?'

'I'll leave it in a little longer in case something happens. I'll take it out before you leave.'

'And what time do we leave?'

'When the ambulance comes. They're probably on their way now. The discharge form is almost ready for your parents to pick up. The date of the next appointment is also written on the file. I think you'll be back in three to four weeks.'

'Wonderful!' I replied ironically. 'And how many more times will I have to come back?'

'Until you are well.'

Every patient who is immobile has the right to request an ambulance from the county of residence to the hospital or vice versa. My parents made a request to The Ambulance Station in Bacău, only things were not exactly as they should have been.

By twelve o'clock the ambulance had arrived. It was in a very bad shape to my dismay, given the conditions I had to endure. The paramedic had to take another patient in the same ambulance. In front were the driver, my mother and the mother of the other patient, who was a child of about one or two, who was in the woman's arms, and in the back, there was me on a stretcher with my father in a seat, surrounded by dozens of pieces of luggage. It was over thirty-five degrees outside, and the vehicle had no air conditioning. This is how a patient with severe central vertebral trauma was transported 300 kilometres, hardly breathing, in 2014. Not to mention the mess that surrounded the stretcher and the gas cylinders that smelled horrible. The ambulance man was not to blame, he was just doing his job. He had been tasked to drive us to Bacău and to bring two patients, but he was not given any details about the patients. It was like two kilograms of potatoes and two patients were the same, there was no difference. I had a hard time on that six-hour journey. I cried for fear, for evil, for everything. I was wet from head to toe, and I felt horrible. My father cooled me down with a fan all the way, but it was still hard for me.

We arrived in front of the block just past six p.m. My aunt was waiting for me with my uncle, Ramo, Sami, Miruna, but there were also some neighbours.

I have lived in that neighbourhood since 2006 and had a great childhood. There were so many children playing together in the summer evenings that our parents could barely get us back inside. Maria and Teodora were my best friends. Magda appeared later in my life, around 2009–2010, when she moved into the same block, and we became closer even later, somewhere in 2011–2012, but I think the friendships with Maria and Teodora was more authentic than the one with Magda, too bad that I realised that too late.

There was a difference of exactly two weeks between Teodora and me. We both had the same star sign of Leo: I was born on the 5th and she on the 19th of August. Maria was a year younger than us, but she was always first with the best ideas. The block of flats I lived in was divided into four staircases. I lived at D, Teo at C, and Maria, in fact, her grandmother, at B. Theoretically, Maria did not live there, her grandparents did, but she spent the summers with them. My father worked twenty-four-hour shifts, and my mother alternated shifts (one week of early shifts when she came home after four p.m., the other of late shifts when she came home after ten p.m.) Form about the age of six, I had had to get used to staying at home alone. At first it was hard for me, but my parents borrowed money and bought me a computer to play on, so time passed faster, and that's how I got used to being alone in the house. I had learned to use the stove, even to make French fries. However, when it got dark, I feared being alone, especially since I lived on the ground floor, so I went to Maria's grandparents. God, how much these people did for me, for us, the trio of Maria, Teo and Andreea. They took us to the park, watched over us so that we wouldn't get hurt, carried our toys, and so much more. When the cherries appeared in the trees next to the block, we would pick them together and Maria's grandmother would make us compote. There were several old ladies on Maria's stairs, but there were also a few on Teo's, and every night they used to gather and sit on the benches in front of stairway B.

'We'll go to the benches to gossip with the old ladies!' I used to say to my parents every afternoon. It was so beautiful. The "old hags", as we called them, always made us laugh, telling us various things about themselves. Mrs Rodica was hilarious; sometimes the discussions with her were perhaps too informative.

God bless her. She died too early of cancer.

In addition to our trio, there were other children, and so we were together in groups all the time. At first, it was just Coco, my neighbour, and Dory, Mrs Cati's nephew (the neighbour my parents and I liked the most), who came from Italy every August. Then the twins Ionuț and Marian moved next door. They also came from other blocks of flats, and in the summer, when we all gathered, there was such a commotion that some nervy neighbours would throw bags of water and shout at us. It is true that we were screaming a bit loudly, and not for an hour or two, but until ten or eleven at night. I was an early bird myself, the first one to go out in the mornings. From nine to ten I would go out and shout for Maria, because I knew that she would wake up early as well, then we would shout together for Teodora. Yes, I was really shouting, not knocking on their door. I would go in front of the stairs and yell "Maria, Mariaa, Măriuța, Teodoraaa, Teeeoo" until someone came to the window. It was easier with Maria as her flat was on the first floor and she could hear me easily, but with Teo I had to prepare my lungs to shout so she could hear me. We even managed to have picnics together by the blocks. Then we played with dolls, took them on walks, threw the ball at the walls of the block, made sand food, coloured the pavements, played skipping, ran until we grazed our elbows and knees, ate fruits we found in the trees and in the evening, we fell asleep – tired out – and did not know what suffering was. We used to play "passes" or "polenta" with the boys and sometimes we would hit the neighbours' windows. At other times, the ball went into the old woman's bedroom on the first floor.

'You stupid kids!' we could hear Mrs Anisoara screaming from the house and then through the window.

'Can you give us the ball back, please? We won't do it again!' we shouted in unison.

'Next time I'll cut it up, and you won't see it again!'

Of course, there were hundreds of other times. Once the ball got stuck on the awning in front of Mrs Anisoara's bedroom window. The canopy was connected to the staircase of the block and the boys climbed up to it to retrieve the ball. It was dangerous. They used the windowsill on the ground floor, where Coco lived, climbed a gas meter and reached the roof. I once jumped from a cover like that, but that's another story.

'Please forgive me, I can't watch this!' Maria's grandmother, Mrs Floarea, told my aunt in tears a few minutes before the ambulance arrived. Everyone was told that I would return in a wheelchair, different from how they knew me.

Oh, of course I burst into tears. While my luggage was being taken out of the ambulance, my relatives greeted me and then Mrs Cati came to the ambulance door to talk to me.

'My baby,' Mrs Cati told me with tears on her cheek.

I knew. It was a great shock, far too big, for those who had known me before to see me like that. Even a dead person looked better than I did then. I was lying on the stretcher, thin, with a very white face and purple hands covered with marks and scars everywhere. I had little hair on my head, and I could barely speak.

'Hello,' I answered crying.

'Don't cry, baby! You'll be fine, I'm convinced of that.'

They pulled the stretcher out of the ambulance and put me in the wheelchair. So many people gathered around me, even strangers, people simply passing through the area. Everyone could see that I was a vegetable, that I was not capable of anything. I gathered all my strength and refrained from crying in front of everyone. I didn't say anything to anyone. I was just waiting anxiously to be taken inside as soon as possible. There were a few steps at the entrance to the block, so my father, uncle and Sami lifted me up in the chair over those steps. I was feeling emotions that are hard to describe. Emotions of revolt, sadness, guilt and a lot of helplessness. I was finally home, after about 120 consecutive days in hospital.

The wheelchair was quite bulky, it only just fitted through the apartment door. When I saw myself in the hallway mirror, I wanted to scream, to yell, to somehow manifest myself so that all the pain that was pressing on my soul would come to the surface. I refrained as much as I could, for fear of making my family even more sad, and only shed a few tears. Our apartment was very small. It was only forty-two metres squared, with two rooms, and modifications had to be made to fit my special bed in the living room. They took more furniture out of the living room and moved it to the bedroom, so you could barely move around. In the living room they left the hospital bed and the sofa for one of my parents to sleep on. Once we were inside the apartment there was not enough space to push the chair, so my father and Sami took me in their arms from the hall straight to the bed.

The bed was made up with everything I needed. It was electric and had a pressure sore mattress, as well as an orthopaedic pillow which helped me to sleep better. The bed frame was not white, like a hospital bed, but brown and even had side panels, which my parents could pull up when they turned me to one side. Because I had no control over my body, when I was turned to one side, I was supported by pillows, so as not to fall on my back, but the pillows could fall if they were not supported by something. So, the panels or bars of the bed were all I needed to lay on my side as comfortably and safely as possible. My mother had asked my aunt to buy new bed linen, and she did and even guessed my favourite colour. She had bought a light blue sheet which I really liked.

After they put me to bed, my mother and aunt started washing me with a towel. A wet towel soaked in soap that they wiped all over my body was in fact me getting a bath. Then they dressed me in pyjamas.

'I hope you're hungry, right?' my mother asked me.

'Yes. Aunty, did you buy me what I asked for?' I replied.

'Sure, honey! Spiral frozen potatoes and sweet ketchup, shall I fry them?'

'Yes please!'

I ate, then my parents started unpacking, while I exchanged a few words with my relatives. It was hard, almost impossible, for me to get used to everything I was going through. I was at home, but not as I would have liked. I was lying in a bed and breathing.

From the window I could hear the voices of young people who had different lives, a life that I had once had too, but which had been taken away from me without my being able to enjoy it for long enough. My soul was crying inside me. When it got dark outside, the relatives all left, and I was left alone with my mother and father. They gave me the medication; my mother emptied my bladder; and then they prepared me for bed. We set a schedule: I was to stay on my back and sleep with my mother in the room until two-thirty, at two-thirty my parents would turn me on my right side and my father would stay with me until six-thirty, when the next bladder drainage had to be done.

When the lights in the house went out and everyone was in bed, I began to cry quietly, as I had learned to do, so that my parents would not hear me. I wasn't crying out loud, only dozens of tears were streaming down my cheeks. I couldn't fall asleep, and my only thought was how I could have been so naive and stupid to get in the car with someone I didn't know anything about. The thought that I had ruined my own life drained me of strength. For that reason, I had no right to complain, to say that I could no longer cope or to give up. I had a moral obligation, especially to my parents, to swallow everything. Somehow, I complied. I started to learn to control myself, to control my emotions and to bottle them inside myself, to say nothing and to suffer in silence.

At two-thirty the alarm went off on the phone. I had stopped crying about half an hour before. My nose was stuffy, but I didn't talk much, and I kept my eyes closed so they wouldn't suspect anything. Anyway, the only light in the room came from a small wall lamp, so there wasn't enough light to see my face. I finally managed to fall asleep after they turned me onto my right side.

In the morning we followed the routine learnt in the hospital with the bladder draining, hygiene and medication, then I ate a yogurt.

'Do you want me to lift your bed up a little?' my mother asked me.

'No, I'm fine like this. Do you have any idea what happened with all my bracelets and accessories I had on the day of the accident?'

'I really do not know. Maybe they are in the bag that the hospital gave us.'

'Did you keep it, as I asked you to?'

'I think so. I asked your aunt not to throw the bag away because you wanted to see the clothes. It should be on the balcony; I'll go and look for it.'

A few days after the accident, when I was in Iaşi, in the ICU, I had asked my mother about the sweatshirt I had on the morning of the tragedy. I knew that they had cut my clothes during the rescue, but I didn't know to what extent they had cut them off. The sweatshirt was not mine and I thought it could be saved so that I could return it. Mum told me then that a nurse from the ICU in Bacău had given her everything I had had on me, but she did not know the condition of the clothes. I asked her to keep everything she received. That's what she did! My mother found the bag on the balcony with all the things I had had on me that morning. She took some pieces of fabric out of the bag. Pieces full of fuel and blood. That strong smell that invaded my nostrils on 27th March had been kept intact in that bag. I didn't have the strength to see everything that was in the bag, and I stopped my mother after looking at several pieces of fabric. As I saw them, the first seconds of that fateful time came to my mind, when I could no longer speak and could barely breathe. Even my bra had been fragmented. The blue ball and chain were intact, exactly as the nurses had left it. The bracelets from my right hand were fine, but the ones from the left were cut and stained with blood. The earrings with gold stars from Turkey, my favourites, were not there. They probably flew out of my ears at the time of the crash. Even the sneakers had signs on them of how terrible the injuries I had received were.

'Thanks. Now you can throw them away. Keep my chain and the good bracelets,' I told my mother.

'Good! Do you need anything else?'

'No, you can go to the kitchen to eat. Just turn off the TV, please. I want peace.'

'Okay, as you wish.'

I was left alone in the room, just me and myself. The TV didn't appeal to me. I was looking at the ceiling and thinking. There was nothing I could do, and time seemed to stand still. I wanted to go back to the hospital. There I saw people and there were things to distract me, and I felt better, but I knew that I had to stay at home for a while. I would have liked to do something with my time, to get on Facebook, to talk to someone, anything to make me get out of this state. Only I couldn't move at all. I couldn't hold a phone in my hand. I couldn't hold a book or turn the pages. I was completely useless.

31

Re-entering life

The 5th of August arrived, my birthday. The time I was supposed to be spending on a trip to France with my dance group. I don't know how the planets aligned but a week before leaving, the trip was cancelled so in some ways I did not miss out. I was surprised by how many people came to see me that day. It wasn't a normal fourteen-year-olds teenager party, and I hoped that my fifteenth birthday would be different. Nonetheless, my parents dressed me nicely in a new neon green shirt and a pair of blue trousers. I still had marks on my hands from the dozens of needles that had pierced my veins, and the bald patches on my scalp were noticeable. It was probably hard for those who knew me as I was before to look at me. I was in the middle of the room, in a bed, and everyone else crowded around me. My relatives, my godparents and Renata, a few school friends and Maria and Teodora crossed the threshold of my house. I hadn't expected so many people, especially Maria and Teo, so it was a lovely surprise. However, someone was missing. Magda, the person to whom I had given the title of best friend was not there. She had a moral duty to be close to me, but she wasn't. She was out of the country, but she could have at least made a phone call. That's what friends do.

I received lots of gifts and about three cakes. It felt like no one knew how to behave around me, how to approach me or what to say. Honestly, I didn't know how to behave either, but I wanted them to look at me the way they did before. I would have liked to tell them, "I haven't changed at all, I'm still the same Andreea as before the 27th of March", but I knew I was fooling myself, because my physical situation made me feel empty. In the evening, the twins from next door, Ionuţ and Marian, came to see me, as well as Dory, Mrs Cati's nephew, who had just arrived from Italy, and Cosmin, a boy from the neighbourhood. They were more relaxed; they did not censor their talk in any way and spoke naturally and openly to me, as if I had no problems. I enjoyed that; it was what I needed. They told me about all the mischief they had got up to. They also told me that Mrs Anişoara and Mrs Veronica, two of our neighbours, had died. I was sorry for them. I had memories of them. Mrs Anişoara's passing away due to her old age I could accept but Mrs Veronica's? I had questions about that. She always spoke nicely to me and complimented me when we met, but behind her smiles there was huge suffering. She had two boys and one of them had taken the wrong path and had unhealthy vices. There was no month in which he would not make a noise on the stairwell and break the windows. I think he was violent with his mother as she often had bruises on her face.

My relatives gave me a tablet as a gift, and the day after my birthday, I tried to use it. I could not. I couldn't hold it in my hand or type on it, but my mother helped me. She sat down next to my bed so that I could see her movements and I told her my email and password for Facebook. I had not been on social media for more than four months and I had missed it. I had about sixty messages and over one hundred friend requests and notifications. My mother didn't know how to use a tablet or Facebook, so I guided her through all the steps. She opened the link where there were dozens of posts about the accident. I didn't read them all, I just glanced at them. The same thing happened with the messages.

They were messages of compassion from different acquaintances, from different friends. Then I asked my mother to turn it off. I was uncomfortable with someone accessing my Facebook account. I had no secrets from my mother, I had told her all the nonsense I had done one evening when I was at Bagdasar Hospital. However, having your mother going through your messages is not very pleasant, especially while you are watching.

I was due to return to the recovery hospital in Bucharest in two weeks. Meanwhile, I passed some tests for promotion to the eighth grade. I have always been concerned with learning, and gaining knowledge is very important to me. At the time of the accident, I already had at least one grade in each subject, but I needed a few more. My teachers came to the house. I was in bed. I didn't have much room for the wheelchair in the living room, but I wouldn't have tolerated it very well anyway. So, the best option was to stay in bed and have each teacher sit in a chair by the bed and keep the books on their lap.

'My dear, that's all. Congratulations! You have officially passed the eighth grade,' the headmistress told me, after the French teacher gave me my final mark.

I couldn't help myself and burst into tears in front of my mother, the class teacher and three other teachers. I was crying with anger and pain because that's not how I wanted to achieve promotion to the eighth grade, the last year of Secondary School. I wanted to be like all my friends – to go to parks, to dance, to have fun, to enjoy life. I was at that age when I had discovered the world, with the conviction that no one and nothing could touch it. But one split second had made me discover how terrible life can be. I had absolutely nothing left to draw my energy from, to extract a drop of power. I struggled and pulled myself together so as not to crash, not to go crazy. My whole present was black and so was my soul. I had experienced things that would be imprinted on my brain for a long time.

During that time, I made myself toughen up, I put aside my prejudices and negative attitude, and I went out twice. It was hard for me to accept because I didn't want people to see me like that, in a wheelchair and completely changed. Going out was complicated not only because of my negative spirit, but also because it was a real physical ordeal for my parents, even though they were happy that I wanted to leave the house. We didn't have room in the apartment to move around in a wheelchair, and that meant my parents had to carry me in their arms from the living room to the hallway. It wasn't too far away, but in a crowded space the whole manoeuvre became harder, especially since I couldn't hold my head and my parents had to pay attention to every detail so as not to hurt me. There were a few steps in front of the block and so we needed a third person to help my parents to lift the wheelchair. Perhaps some of you will say that there are techniques for going up and down the stairs with a wheelchair. Yes, there are, but those manoeuvres cannot be used with any wheelchair, only the lightest ones. My chair was very bulky and had lots of attachments on it, and we didn't even know about those techniques at the time. I didn't know a lot of things, but I gradually learned them from others. We didn't really have anyone to call on during the day. By midday, most of the neighbours were at work. So, my father would bring the car to the front of the block, next to the stairs, and my poor parents would carry me all the way from the living room to the car. It was not an easy mission at all.

Going by car for the first time made my heart pound. I had been driven in ambulances many times, but then I was on the stretcher, and I couldn't see the traffic around me. Going by ambulance had also been hard, and I had barely got used to staying calm and not feeling scared. Every time we braked, or we went over a pothole, the stretcher jolted forward, making me feel like I would shoot off it. Now, I had to sit in the front seat, to my father's right. Honestly, I felt safer in the car seat, held by the seat belt, than in the wheelchair. When we began driving and saw the cars in the traffic, I felt that they were all coming towards us, and we would have an accident. I closed my eyes, but it made it worse. I started to cry, to scream, to tell my father to stop, but then I took a deep breath, as best I could, and I thought, "I must face this fear, because I'm in good hands." My father was always an attentive and prudent driver and had over twenty years of driving experience. I trusted him, that was not my problem. But I was thinking that the other drivers might make mistakes, as Alex did.

The first outing was to Kaufland for shopping. In a way, I felt good. I hadn't seen my city in almost five months. The summer air caressed my face, and the sun's rays coloured my skin a little. However, the curious looks of the people who saw me made me feel like an alien, like a creature with three heads and six hands. I wore a short-sleeved blouse, because it was summer and hot outside, so I had a lot of scars in plain sight. I thought about what the people staring at me might be thinking. Most of them saw me as disabled, of course, and that thought made me shiver. In fact, labelling me like that bothered me the most, because our education and society, in general, tends to label people by appearances, rather than judging the real person. I would have liked to go and tell them, "Don't look at me like that, you are hurting me even more! A bloody car accident did this."

When I got home, I felt sick and had a terrible headache. Some would say that I was cursed, but I don't have much to do with ideas like that or superstitions, although some things have happened to me which have left me speechless about the way the Universe works. For example, the night before the fateful accident, I went out with Diana, a school friend of Magda's, to pick up Magda from the bus station. She had come from Botosani by minibus. After we picked up Magda, we returned to my neighbourhood and stayed in a small park located about 150 meters from the block where I lived. We chatted a while and I accepted Magda's proposal to go with her the next day to see Alex. Under these circumstances, I needed an excuse to justify my absence from school the next day. I needed a good excuse, especially since it was the class teacher's birthday and we had prepared for that day in detail. And guess what idea came to my mind? Because I had a bad kind of gastritis when I was six or seven, which recurred several times, it occurred to me to announce that I had to go to Iaşi, for a check-up for this problem. The irony of fate was such that I did arrive in Iaşi the next day, not in any ordinary way, but almost dying. Should I mention the nine black cats that crossed my path in the 150 meters of my journey home?

Let me also say that a few days before the accident, after school, I went to the Subway Pub with a group of so-called friends, and a girl who was doing vlogging asked me to help her with the filming of the new video for her vlog. She picked me out from all the people that were there? It was a video in which she talked about people with disabilities and the fact that most of them are very independent and offer society valuable contributions, despite the obstacles they encounter. I liked the way she spoke, but of course, the words went in through one ear and came out through the other. It may sound strange, but now, putting all the signs together, things connect. Maybe if I didn't treat everything superficially and I wasn't so naive, I could have prevented this misfortune –maybe not. Should I also mention the signs that my parents had, especially my mother, who personally makes me shiver when I hear her telling them? No, I won't say any more.

The second time I went out to Subway, a charity concert was being organised for me. At first, I didn't want to go, but a voice in my head told me that it would be nice to be there too, at least out of respect for those who had helped me and continued to help me. It was overwhelming enough to go back there. Before the accident, I spent most of February in Subway. And in March I went there a few times. When I entered, I felt like crying. I could see myself in every place in the room. Every moment I spent in that pub came to mind. I saw myself as I had been before 27th March, happy and enjoying every moment. After more people gathered, the concert organised by the singing club, that included Miruna, Ramona's daughter, started. About four people sang, then I saw Ramona walking up to the front. She had a speech to make. "Until 27th March, we did not know how privileged we are, those of us who can get out of bed in the morning ..." I couldn't listen to anymore because I burst into tears and told my family that I wanted to leave. They understood and took me out of Subway. On the way home, I asked my father to take us to the street where I had had the accident. I wanted to see the place where my life had changed. The place that robbed me of all traces of happiness. The place where most of me perished. The place where all my ideals were shattered. The place where I lost everything. Absolutely everything.

32

Alba Iulia

On 24th August, I returned to the hospital. Once again, I became the person who rejected everyone, cried and barely uttered a few words. The urinary tract infection came back as did the fever. I was fed up with medications, injections and IVs. I felt like throwing up just from the smell, and I knew them even blindfolded. I no longer had serious breathing problems so this time I didn't stay in the ICU, but in a normal ward. A screaming two-year-old baby who was just learning to crawl on all fours, and a rather irresponsible mother, were all I needed to make me tense and unapproachable when I was already on edge. The child had neuro developmental delay, which was noticed a bit late by his family. He was only just learning to crawl now, at the age of two, after being in the recovery unit. Alberto's mother was quite young. She sat with her phone in her hand all day and didn't talk much to the child. The poor child was just giggling and saying "Papapa", meaning "goodbye".

The late evenings on that ward were the most trying. I had a fever of 39.5°c, and in delirium was gazing and following the dots on the ceiling. Alberto was crawling around on the floor, slamming the bed drawers and screaming in his own language. When his mother put him to bed, he slapped the wall with his palms shouting "Papapa". I flinched again and again. I was so worn out by the noise. My mother argued with the woman because she didn't do anything for Alberto, she didn't pay any attention to her son and let him do just what he wanted. That experience, but also others like that, helped to mould me and increased my patience. Over the years, Alberto grew up, started walking, and went to be looked after by his grandmother. His mother had continued in the same irresponsible way she had behaved when we first met.

After two weeks of recovery spent at the Robănescu Hospital in Bucharest, I returned home on Friday evening, and on Sunday morning I left for Alba Iulia, a private recovery centre. Not having much experience with therapists and the recovery process, I still didn't know how to compare one centre with another, what makes one better or worse, what might help me or not, but we, my parents and I, were desperate to find something or someone to heal me. So, any recommendation we heard, we went for it.

In a way, the therapy in Alba Iulia was beneficial to me. I worked intensively, even if I did not make significant progress. However, the recovery therapies were not as numerous as at Robănescu's, and the equipment was not very varied. We also ran into some obstacles. The centre was not a hospital. The accommodation was about 750–800 meters away from the centre in an ordinary block of flats which was inaccessible for a person in a wheelchair. It may be that this arrangement was easier for the other people who came with children, as they were small, most of them born with cerebral palsy, but it was very difficult for my parents. I was the oldest of the patients in the centre and the only one affected by a car accident. The accommodation block did not have a ground floor, it only had a basement and upper floors, so inevitably there were stairs, many stairs. We stayed in the basement. Every day, my parents carried me in their arms tens of meters, from the bedroom to the front of the block, going down and up many steps. They would take the chair to the front of the block, then take me, and on the way back after a day of treatment, they would take me out of the chair and carry me in their arms to the bed. It was extremely hard for us all, and my parents' backs got hurt as a result of going through hundreds of manoeuvres. A paralysed person is rigid, their limbs are like a stone. I had a little active mobility in my hands, and they were easier to handle. However, my legs had zero power. They were dead weights, like they are with dead people, only I also had an accentuated spasticity (muscle rigidity), which made any movement more difficult.

In addition to the huge problem with the stairs, it was difficult for my parents to help with the sleeping arrangements. The centre did not have a special hospital-type bed, but an ordinary double bed. My parents had to improvise so we could get some rest. In other words, it was better at home, but all these barriers were not reasons to give up. We adapted and focused on the purpose for which we were there.

I was happiest when I managed to take a bath. A normal bath, in the bathtub, because until then a bath had meant a wet towel soaked in soap. At home there was not enough space for my parents to put me in the bathtub. Of course, this wasn't a bath like it had been before the accident. I had no stability and my parents had to hold me up. My father held my back while my mother washed me. Although my body was in the water, I could not feel anything from my neck down. I couldn't feel that pleasant sensation created by the warm water, nor the foam that cleansed my body, but the fact that I was there and doing that meant a lot. Before the accident, washing in the bathtub seemed normal to me, a natural action that everyone does, but now I was looking at the situation from a different perspective.

I got along well with the therapists at the centre even if I was still unapproachable and resistant at first. I did physiotherapy with Mrs Elena, a Transylvanian woman. I gave her a lot of headaches, especially when she put me in the vertical holder. The upright holder was a device that lifted me to my feet. Everything was passive, the device kept me in that position, and I was tied with several straps. I was scared to stay in it and it gave me a strange feeling. The verticaliser played an important role in blood circulation. For almost half a year I had lain on my back, only sitting up for short bursts; my blood was no longer circulating properly. This device mimicked the vertical position for thirty minutes and helped with my blood flow. Well, it wasn't really thirty minutes and I never made it to ninety degrees, because in the first seconds after getting up I saw black in front of my eyes, I felt sick and I started to shake, but I managed to endure up to sixty-five to seventy degrees, on good days, for an interval of fifteen to twenty minutes.

Coming to the centre in Alba Iulia also meant learning about its story. The centre was born through the suffering of some parents. Their little girl was born with cerebral palsy. All the money in the world could do nothing for her. All the money in the world could not make her live the life of a normal child. The child was six years old, but she could not speak, she could not call for her parents, she could not walk, she could not even sit. It was that kind of harsh lesson which makes you re-analyse your life and realise how lucky you are.

'I spent tens, hundreds of thousands of euros and did everything that I heard of. When it made no difference, I felt robbed! Then I realised that this was our cross to bear, mine and my wife's. I started tentatively and got here today. I did everything you see in this centre. We brought in therapists, we bought devices and we have managed to help dozens of children. Even if we didn't manage to do anything for our daughter, we are glad to have her alive,' the owner of the centre told my father.

We went to that centre several times, then gave up because we had to struggle too much with the accommodation, but that doesn't mean it's not a good centre. It just didn't suit my condition and my trauma. Not forgetting that the therapists there, through their work, have healed hundreds of children.

33

Unexpected friendship

Until December, my time was shared between Bucharest, Alba Iulia and home school. I didn't think for a second to "freeze" my year, even though my physical condition was not great and I didn't feel well mentally either. When the school year started, I kept thinking about my classmates, how much fun they would be having. It was the final year of secondary school. I was fourteen years old and theoretically should have been starting that wonderful period of life – adolescence. I had begun to experience a little of that before I was hit by suffering, but I did not have much time to enjoy it.

Every day, at least one teacher came to my house. I lay in bed, and they sat on the chair next to my bed, with the books on their laps. It must have been a difficult psychological threshold for them to overcome. In order for me to learn, my mother read my textbooks to me several times and I had to memorise what she said. I had a hard time getting used to this style, but I pulled myself together as much as I could. I didn't intend to neglect my studies. They have always been important to me.

With each passing day, I missed more and more. I missed the evening walks in the park. I missed my dance classes. School hours. Fun during breaks. Jokes made by my classmates. I missed people. I missed happiness. I missed everything. Magda hadn't been my only option to spend my days with, but I was attached to her. I'd had other friends, maybe it was fate that made me so committed to her, although I'm not at all reconciled with this idea.

Christmas was approaching and Magda had only visited me a few times. I was disappointed by her attitude towards me. I was disappointed that she wasn't the person I thought she was. I had always been by her side, no matter what, whether she was right or wrong, and now that I needed her more than ever, she turned her back on me. I don't even know if she was sorry for what had happened, if she had remorse or if she had even comprehended the situation. Judging by her attitude, she didn't seem to be affected in any way. I don't blame her for the accident, but she did contribute. She didn't pressure me, but somehow she had influenced me, and so plunged me into this suffering. I can't help but think about what would have happened if I hadn't agreed to go with her. I can't help but think about how things might have been if, before she left Botosani, the day before the accident, when she called me and told me what she was going to do the next day, I had told her that I couldn't go with her, because at nine o'clock we were going to celebrate the birthday of the class teacher; if, later, when she arrived in Bacău and we met up, she asked me to come with her again and I agreed. I can't help but think how happy I could have been if only I had been more confident in myself and my decisions.

Magda had disappointed me the most because she was the person I had the highest expectations of. However, there were other people close to me who did the same. I never judged them. I don't know how I would have behaved if I had been in their place, but I hope I would have done things a little differently. Instead, a surprise came from someone I didn't expect.

Mara, who I had shared a desk with at school, was the only person who took an interest in me, looked out for me and visited me often. We had known each other for two years out of the six, since I moved to Alecsandri secondary school. At the end of sixth grade, we started talking more and became closer, and we even saw each other several times that summer. We weren't always desk buddies, because the class teacher kept separating us, but we often stayed together, even during breaks. She told me her secrets and I told her mine, only I was more reserved, I was not as open with her as she was with me. I saw her as a good partner, and that was all, I would never have counted on her. But she proved me wrong. She proved to me that she is a fair person and a faithful and trustworthy friend.

Mara's parents were separated, as were Magda's parents. But education made a difference. Education always makes a difference. Mara lived with her mother and grandmother. A grandmother of the sort you rarely meet in life, a special person, who on the only visit I made to Mara made me feel like I lived in their house and I was one of the family members, and a mother who, although single, had educated the child in the most comprehensive and beautiful way. The proof of this was amply displayed in Mara's behaviour towards me after the accident. She didn't owe me anything, unlike Magda. She could have chosen the easy way and disappeared, as they all did, but she wanted to be different. She wanted to show her quality and morality, and for that I thank her.

December was very overwhelming. For most people it is one of the most beautiful and long-awaited months of the year, but at that time, I would have liked it to disappear from the calendar. For me it was the first holiday where I was paralysed, and this triggered a lot of emotions in me. I resented people's happiness. I was bitter about everyone's special moments, I was a prisoner in my body, stuck between four walls. Lots of people visited me that month, most of them relatives and acquaintances of my parents and a few colleagues. Some friends who I expected didn't even give me a call, and others only bothered to write to me on Facebook asking if I had recovered. It felt like they didn't care how I was or if I needed anything, they just wanted to know if I had started walking. I asked my mother to answer them because I still couldn't use the tablet. When they saw the negative answer, many did not even bother to write back.

This was another harsh reality – the fact that only my parents were really committed to me. It was hard to understand that my friends had disappeared from my landscape to take care of their own lives, and that I was left alone, with no shoulder to cry on. I couldn't load my parents with even more, and I couldn't burden Mara with everything I was thinking. I was afraid she would walk away too. I was happy that she was telling me about the outside world and in this way I felt at least involved in a social life. But I wanted more. I wanted to have more people around me and not feel so alone anymore. I perceived loneliness as a boulder, which crushed my soul, made me question my existence and feel completely useless.

The wish for the New Year was, of course, for my life to return to normal, and for me to become Andreea again, the girl before 27th of March. To return to the person who wholeheartedly enjoyed every moment. The person who felt happiness in every gesture, who could do whatever she wanted. The person who was healthy and could feel every part of her body.

34

My second home

At the start of January, I returned to the recovery hospital in Bucharest. I hadn't made much physical progress since July. I had some mobility in my right arm. The left arm also showed a few signs, more on the sensitivity side. The rest of my body was totally stiff. To move forward, I needed finger mobility, which was completely absent. Even the strength in the active muscles was not as I expected, as I believed the recovery would ensure. I only had about a fifth of the strength in my muscles. What I could do for myself was extremely limited. My body was still frozen. I thought that as I regained my sensitivity and motor activity, they would come back like new, like before the spinal cord injury, but it wasn't like that. I had to start from scratch, more like a new-born. I had a lot of work to do to even to move my hand to my mouth.

Robănescu Hospital had become our second home. Although I was in a hospital, in a place that many fear, I liked staying there more than staying at home. It was harder for my parents because they had to shuttle their lives between two places. But I liked being in hospital because I was surrounded by people. Since October, I had developed a beautiful friendship with a girl called Natalia and her mother, Mrs Mari. I asked the nurses to put us in the same room if we were ever in hospital at the same time. Natalia, who was almost thirteen, also had an impressive story.

In 2013, when she was only eleven, a car accident stole her childhood and the smile from her face. A bone in her skull had been crushed and she had been in a coma for some time. The doctors did not give her mother any hope, and one even dared to tell her, "Take her home, madam! Do you think that vegetables recover?" When she woke up, Natalia was no longer the child her parents knew. She was no longer the eleven-year-old who knew every verse from the epic poem called *"The bright star"* (*Luceafarul* by Mihai Eminescu – the most famous Romanian poet) and took the best prizes in competitions. In time, she recovered ninety-eight per cent physically, but mentally she was left with the effects of the crash. She can no longer speak or think as before, she will no longer be awarded prizes at school competitions, but she has won another prize, which is above all. She won her battle with life. She has won a chance that not many have. Mrs Mari fought side by side with Naty, even though she sometimes struggled doing it alone – her husband did not know how to keep the vow he made on their wedding day ("I will love you for better or worse") and left her. Now, Naty is eighteen years old and she is a real young lady. She will be in the eleventh grade in the fall and she certainly won't stop there. She speaks and concentrates with difficulty, but she will never give up enjoying what she has.

Mrs Laura, the psychologist I went to and loved more and more, organised a social group with all the teenagers in the hospital. The idea for the group came in October. Initially I was not very happy about it. Although it was a group for teenagers, I took my mother along with me because I constantly felt like crying. To calm down I had to drink water, which I could not do on my own. Going to the group every day, I developed more control, and by January I was already more emotionally stable. The social group had a big impact on me. We were quite a large group and we continued to see each other even outside of meeting times. Usually, we would gather in the evenings in the wards where those without parents were staying. Only a few others used a wheelchair, my case being one of the worst of those in the group. The rest were less severe, with scoliosis, kyphosis, and various other physical conditions from birth or other trauma.

Andrei was also in a wheelchair. He had fallen from a tree a few months before and suffered a spinal cord injury. His lower limbs had been affected. He has been somewhat abandoned since he was a child, and even in difficult times his parents were not close to him. He was taken care of by Marian, a nineteen-year-old boy, who was a positive influence on me. Getting to know everyone did me a great deal of good. Knowing that I always had someone close to me to talk to was another boost for my morale. I laughed, I joked, as if I was beginning to see life with different eyes, to see a patch of colour in my present full of suffering. I no longer attached so much importance to the pains and difficult conditions that were trying me, and I tried to pull myself together as much as possible.

'Why is it so noisy in here? Come on, everyone in their wards now! Young man, don't you see what time it is? Visits are allowed until nine p.m., what are you doing here?' Mrs Olga, the fiercest nurse, came badgering us one evening.

'Excuse us, madam, I'm leaving right away,' Marian replied.

Indeed, it was past ten p.m., but it was a pleasant atmosphere and neither of us left. Mrs Olga was not a bad person. But she was strict. She didn't accept compromises. In a way, she was just doing her job. She was responsible for all the children who did not have a companion, and this made her very attentive to everything that was going on.

Because of the social group and the people there, I only wanted to stay at the hospital, I did not want to return home, but because that was the rule, I accepted it, and I was glad when my mother read on the discharge note that the next hospitalisation was going to be right next month, in February.

35

Judgement

On the nights when sleep had forgotten me, I searched my mind
for all sorts of solutions that might make me more independent.
The first solution was to ask my father to buy me a bed table.
I had got used to the "bed technology" and, instead of lying
horizontally with my eyes on the ceiling during the day, I started
sitting with my torso raised to seventy-five degrees, sometimes
even ninety. I thought that sitting in that position, with a table
on my lap, I might be able to use the tablet alone. I couldn't move
my fingers, but I could make elbow and shoulder movements, and
in that way I could put my little finger on each key. Dad found a
bed table, and they put it on my lap. He opened my tablet, but it
wasn't as easy as I had imagined. The tablet was too big for me. I
couldn't make big enough movements to reach every corner of the
tablet with my hand. I needed something smaller, like a phone.
However, the touchscreen phone that I had was broken in the
accident, and my parents only had old fashioned, button phones.

My parents acted right away. They dressed me and took me
to Altex (a shop for electronics). They did not think twice about
whether they had enough money for this investment. They just
wanted to bring a smile to my face. I returned with an S3 Neo
and my heart was pounding. In the store I couldn't figure out if I
could use the phone or not. All I knew was that I needed a phone
that was neither too big nor too small. It would also be about

practice. They changed me and put me back to bed, then they lifted my torso and set up the table with the phone. It was the first time in eleven months that I was able to do an action on my own. The phone matched perfectly with my reduced mobility and the way I typed and swiped. By making arm movements I could bring my little finger over the key I needed, and with the help of my forearm movements I let my hand down so that my little finger could touch the screen. I can't put into words the happiness I felt. In those moments I was no longer interested in not being able to walk and not being able to move at all, I was simply very happy with what I had, with the fact that I had managed to use the phone by myself.

I downloaded various applications, including Facebook, and a few games. I could finally read the messages and posts on Facebook from the days after the accident in peace. The news of my accident was covered by several local newspapers and lots of fundraisers had been set up for me.

Among the words of compassion were the comments of other people who humiliated me and made me feel like trash. In difficult times you expect people to be with you, to support you or to do nothing. But in reality, people judge your every move, even after you die. "Thirteen-year-old girl paralysed by the accident caused by a sixteen-year-old teenager" was the headline of the news on most sites. Even worse, someone had written an article entitled "Who is to blame? The girl or the teenager?" I read comment by comment utterly amazed and I could hardly refrain from crying with resentment and revulsion. Some people said that speeding was the cause and that Alex had recovered his license and was driving a month or less after the event. Oh, yes, this is justice in our country, and human judgment was no better. His permit was returned much faster than required by law, but when you have good contacts, it doesn't matter what you do or the seriousness of the deed.

Others trashed and smeared me. "A bitch, she got what she was looking for", "If she needed boys, now she should be full", "She was looking for trouble!", "If she was a good girl she wouldn't end up like that", "Whore!", "She wasn't a good girl anyway", and many more.

It hurt to read all those comments and to find out what some people thought about me. Of course, those people who insulted me never knew me personally, maybe they knew me by sight and that's it. They didn't really know me, but judging is free and some people really like to do it, even when there is a critical situation in the middle. Certainly not going to school that day was not the right choice and I do not encourage skipping school, although everyone does it. It was not a good decision for me to accept the "tour of the town centre" with Alex. I admit that I was not the key to the church, and I did some things that I am not very proud of, but I was never a "slut" or a "whore". I wasn't the one to go from club to club or be seen getting with different boys on benches or in stairwells. By no means have I done anything to deserve being called names like that, I don't think anyone does.

I was not the most obedient child, but neither was I the naughtiest. I had been to the club twice before the accident. Once when I slept at Magda's, we jumped from the first floor and again when I went to the party after the freshman ball at Magda's high school.

Two good and nice boys, the same age as Magda, whom we had known for more than a year, invited us to go with them to a club. I don't think Magda's father would have let us go if we had asked his permission, even though she was fifteen. I was younger and he certainly wouldn't have agreed. So, we thought that at nine-thirty p.m. we would put on our pyjamas and tell them that we were going to sleep so that they would not bother us anymore. Then we started to put on make-up, straighten our hair and get dressed, ready to go out.

It was the first time that I had been to a club and I didn't know how these things worked. Would I be allowed in? Would someone check my ID? I was relying on the fact that my face didn't look like a thirteen-year-old's and that I might readily be taken to be fourteen or fifteen. I didn't even know what to wear, but I didn't care, because I only had jeans, a shirt and a T-shirt, so I wore that. Magda wore a similar outfit, and after we were both ready we had to wait for the lights in the house to go out. Initially, we wanted to go out through the door, but for that, Magda's father and his partner had to fall asleep so they wouldn't hear us. We waited about half an hour and when we saw the light still on, we looked for another way out. We thought about climbing out of the window. Magda's flat was on the first floor, and there was a canopy on the window of her bedroom which we could climb down. It was exactly like the canopy from Aunt Anişoara's window, where the ball got stuck when we were little. However, we sent a message to the boys to come and help us, just in case, and because I was afraid of falling. They came and in absolute silence we climbed down and left.

We went to Club 33, but we didn't stay there long because it was too crowded, then we went to City Pub. Although the situation seems out of the ordinary for a girl of only thirteen years old, I did nothing to put myself in a bad light. I was in the club, and I just danced, and then sat on a chair watching others dance when I was tired. Eighty per cent of the time I only danced with Magda. I didn't drink, I didn't make a fool of myself, I just minded my own business.

I had three so-called childhood relationships, which did not last more than a few days. In these I discovered what it's like to kiss a boy and hold his hand, nothing more. Otherwise, of course, I was in a gang with several girls and boys, but I only socialised with them, I had no other business with the boys. I skipped school several times, with my classmates and by myself. Most of the time I skipped from sports classes, especially when it was hot outside. I didn't skip for anything special. I liked going to Cancicov Park, which was close to the college, and sitting on a bench in peace. The first time I skipped school was at the end of the sixth grade, when I skipped religion class and my friends took me to Studio to drink a juice and eat a cake.

I started putting on make-up just before I turned twelve, about two years before the accident. Sanda, a classmate, helped me apply the make-up for the first time, and because I liked the way I looked, I started to take foundation and mascara from my mother to use. At the time, I didn't use makeup every day. In the seventh grade, it became part of my daily routine. I also liked to dress nicely, to be elegant, wherever I went. I didn't really have sporty or oversized outfits, I preferred fitted clothes.

I sometimes talked ugly, I swore. I judged by appearance or by hearsay. I was critical of others. Sometimes I spoke badly to my parents. I also lied a few times about my identity. There were a few people who thought that I was Magda's half-sister and that we were the same age, or that I was fourteen or fifteen years old. I also had a vice. A colleague taught me to smoke. Normal cigarettes, nothing else. I believed myself to be more interesting by doing all these things. It seemed "fashionable" to me. I liked to sit outside after dark, lie on a bench, look at the starry sky, and smoke a cigarette. That's how I spent the last Sunday before the disaster. I remember every moment of that day, as if it were a movie.

One day, as Magda was in Botoşani, I went out with Diana, a friend of Magda's from school and a neighbour, and during the day other people joined us and we walked through the park until late. We looked at the stars and made our plans for the next weekend, which I was not going to live through in the same physical condition. I usually got back home before nine p.m., no later than ten p.m. during the long summer days. I used to spend time in the mall or in the cafes. I didn't really get a chance to go to parties.

These were my only "debauched" deeds in the years when I knew happiness. I'm not proud of them, but I can't say I'm sorry for them either. If I had known I would have the accident, I would have experienced more, to be honest. I would have liked to know even more and live even more intensely. The rest of my time was spent studying, working on homework and watching movies on the computer. I was not an exemplary girl, but I was not as some people described me in the comments posted on the articles about the accident. A few acquaintances jumped to my defence.

But here, too, someone was missing. Magda didn't write anything in reply to those comments, she just liked them. She was the one who knew me best and knew my true value, but she didn't write a word. This proved to me once again that I really didn't mean anything to her and what happened to me didn't affect her in any way. After looking through all the news and comments, I turned off the wi-fi and asked my parents to lower the bed so I could go back to lying flat. I needed a break from everything I had read.

People are always trying to judge you. They judge by the way you dress or the way you appeared in front of them for a few seconds. They also judge you by the people you sit next to, on the principle that if there is a rotten apple in a basket, the other apples will get damaged too, a maxim that is not 100 per cent valid. Some also judge you if you are thin or fat, if you have freckles or not, if you have crooked or straight teeth, or if you wear clothes from the mall or the cheap market. Social media means that people are getting worse and judging your every move, and if you are looked upon as an impressive person, they can't wait for you to make mistakes so they can throw you to the wolves. If you are sick, they will judge you. And if you're healthy, they judge you. People also judge you when you change your look, when you are happy or sad, when you buy something new or put on an old blouse until the next pay day. They judge you by appearances, without waiting to meet you. If you are unlucky enough to go through a very difficult period that leaves visible signs, not only do people judge you, but they also exclude you from social life. But why all this and for what? We came to earth out of love, out of God's love for people, and instead of being kind, loving each other and helping each other, we make fun of everything we have and tend to destroy those around us. However, the judgment of reckless people who do not have the patience to really know you should not negatively influence or demoralise you. That's what I learned from the lesson I received. Maybe some pointed a finger at me and condemned me, but I always knew my worth and never struck back.

36

The two most beautiful weeks of the year

A year after the event that turned my life upside down, I received some hopeful news. For some time, my cousin had been talking to a recovery clinic in Germany. However, admission there for a few months cost 90,000 euros, an impossibly exorbitant amount for my family – a modest family, who barely managed to cover the medical expenses that were being paid monthly for my existence, plus the regular household expenses that had to be paid. Every month I went to the hospital in Bucharest or to the private clinic in Alba Iulia. Some months I went to both. I stayed in Bucharest for two weeks, then came home on Friday night. On Saturday my parents took my clothes out of my suitcase and washed, dried and packed them again, and on Sunday morning I went to Alba Iulia for another two weeks. For one month, the costs amounted to 6,000 lei, around 1,000 pounds, just for recovery and medical supplies. Of course, people from all over the country, known and unknown, helped us, and the Always Close Foundation from Antena 1 TV station supported us. People may help you once, twice, ten times but they can't do it all the time. The more time passed, the fewer donations there were, and to raise 90,000 euros seemed like an impossible dream.

Then, hope came from the Always Close Foundation at Antena 1 TV station. On 1st April 2015, they called and asked us to attend a live show in Bucharest. For fifteen minutes I was on

TV in front of hundreds of thousands of people who mobilised extraordinarily and gave me another chance at a better and independent life, or at least that is what the people at the clinic in Germany promised about their medical services. Within a few days I found out that the necessary money had been raised, and the next step was to talk to the clinic so they could receive me as soon as possible. I got some malicious comments from this TV appearance too. Some people said that I raised that money to get rich. No, no one gets rich from the campaigns organised on TV, all the money goes to the predetermined goal. I did not receive that money in my hand, that is not what happens. The foundation transferred the money to the account provided by the hospital abroad.

Until things got moving with the departure to Germany, I returned to the hospital in Bucharest. Easter had passed once more. I stayed on the ward with Naty and her mother, but also with Marija, a thirteen-year-old girl who had scoliosis. There were many teenagers in the social group, including Daniela and Ionuț, also with scoliosis, who I became friends with. Although Andrei was no longer hospitalised, Marian continued to visit. Sometimes he would bring Andrei, but he would also come alone. All the medical staff knew him.

We met in January, and after that he came to sit with me every day, and when it was warmer outside, we went out in front of the hospital. He was a ray of light in those hard times. He was the person who I could approach about any subject without hesitation. I think those two weeks I was in the hospital, surrounded by so many people, were the two most beautiful weeks of the year.

We went out in groups every afternoon and walked around the hospital. I enjoyed this so much, as I didn't go out much at home, I didn't have friends at home, and that's what I missed the most.

Andrei came to Marian's house over the weekend. The two had known each other since December, when they met at the hospital, and Marian stayed with Andrei afterwards. Rather than staying in the house to chat, they decided to come to the hospital. They had a plan for all of us to go to the Children's Town, a large park, two bus stops away. I was the only one in a wheelchair, the rest were on foot. If I had refused to expose myself before then, for fear of the way that some people would look at me as a weirdo or as an inferior person, now I accepted the boys' proposal right away. I asked my mother to dress me to go out, and Daniela and Marija put on makeup and arranged my hair. I still had missing hair on my head and bald patches, and at the back I only had a few new strands, but the girls managed to give my hair a little volume. Dressed and arranged nicely, I felt as if I was another person, at least that's how I saw myself in the mirror.

When everyone was ready, we left. The group was made up of Naty, Marija, Daniela, Marian, Ionuţ, Alex and me, as well as the two mothers, mine and Natalia's, who followed us. Walking the streets of Romanian cities is a real challenge for a wheelchair user and their companion. I couldn't push my own wheels anyway, but I was thinking about those who can: how can they manage to climb the dozens of high and uneven kerbs every fifteen meters, or how do their companions cope. My chair was bulky and heavy, and at each kerb one person lifted me from one side and another from the other side. Granted not everyone's chairs are as large and heavy as mine, making this an easier task for some, but what do we do for those in situations like mine? We don't do anything. Nobody does anything. Not even those in charge of infrastructure.

I had never been to such a large park before. There were some high octane fairground rides, various restaurants and food stalls. In the distance, you could see a lake. We walked for several hours through the endless and crowded streets of the park. The boys enjoyed some funny rides with mixed feelings. I felt good in their company, but my mind kept flying to the hundreds of "Why me?" questions, especially when I saw the others around me having fun. In the evening, before we returned to the hospital, we went into Mega Image supermarket to do some shopping, then we ordered pizza and sat down to talk. Staying at the hospital had become more like going on a camp for me. Although we did a lot of therapies, which always reminded me of the real purpose of my stays there, when I returned to the ward it was different. It was getting harder and harder for me to go home, because I knew what awaited me. It was getting harder and harder for me to accept going back to solitude and being marooned between four walls.

When I returned home, I had another sacrifice to face. We had received the answer from the clinic in Germany stating that I was due to be hospitalised on 8th June. I was in the eighth grade at the time, and at the end of June I had the aptitude test for high school admission. I had to forfeit the exam and choose whether I wanted to repeat the year and take the test next year or if I agreed to go into the third round at the beginning of September to a high school where there were vacancies. That meant accepting going to one of the most mediocre high schools; me, someone who was enrolled in one of the best colleges in town. The type of school was not guaranteed either. I could end up in a tech high school, and that was completely against my aims. I cried for many nights, thinking about what to do. My reasoning was that I couldn't do anything, because the appointment was made. I chose not to lose the year and to accept assignment in the third round, with the consolation that regardless of the quality of the high school, at least the option of studying natural sciences would be guaranteed. I put my recovery first, because I had it in my mind that I would return from Germany walking, sound and healthy.

I communicated my decision to the teachers and those from the school inspectorate, who supported me and approved the decision.

37

Graduation and moving on

'On the 5th of June we will have the gymnasium graduation ball, your class can't wait to see you,' my teacher told me during a Romanian literature class.

'I'm not coming,' I answered.

'What do you mean?'

'I'm not attending, simply no way. I don't want anyone to see me like this again. If I get well by then, I'll come, otherwise I won't.'

'I say you should think about it.'

'I have nothing to think about.'

I was fed up with the happiness of others. I couldn't bear to see others smile and be happy. I couldn't bear to watch TV anymore, because even there I only saw milk and honey. The phone didn't appeal to me anymore. I studied for the school exams and I could not find any activity to distract or interest me. I talked a little with the therapist who came daily to do my physiotherapy at home, but that too had started to bore me. My life had become a struggle, which made me more and more tired every day. I hadn't progressed at all in more than a year, I was only accumulating physical and mental exhaustion. It was recommended that I did physical therapy at home, and I did, from the moment I first got home after the accident. In the middle of May we went to the centre in Alba Iulia, and when we returned I realised that I wanted to go to the prom. I realised that regardless of the situation, memories form us, and the gymnasium graduation ball was a moment I would never experience again.

'I've changed my mind, I'm coming to the prom too,' I told my teacher in our penultimate Romanian class.

'Wonderful, that's what I hoped you would decide,' she answered.

It was almost a week before the ball and I had no idea what to wear. I was already very selective in choosing my clothes and now I was constrained by the situation. I agreed to go to the mall (which was the only wheelchair-accessible store) to look for a dress. I finally found one that I liked, but I couldn't try it on in the store. I had gained at least ten kilograms since the accident, so I took my mother's body as a benchmark and let her try on the dress. It was too small for her, but I had to decide whether to get it because the day of the prom was approaching. I chose to buy it because I really liked the way it looked, and my mother went to a seamstress to get the zipper adjusted.

A day before the prom, my father collected the dress from the tailor's shop. I wanted to try it on to see how it suited me. My family struggled to dress me for about half an hour. Dressing an immobilised person – especially in a dress – is a real challenge. When we had finally got the dress on, I found out that it was too big. The change made by the seamstress according to my mother's measurements didn't fit my body. I started to cry out of hatred for the situation. I felt that all the evils of the world were pursuing me and were going to torture me from now until the end of time. It was a miracle that saved the situation, as my desperate mother made dozens of calls to find a seamstress willing to come to the house and fit my dress to my size by the next morning.

Nevertheless, despite all the constraints, we managed to go to the prom. I tried to smile at my colleagues and teachers, but it was too hard a mission. The girls were all nicely dressed, like young ladies. Most of them wore short dresses and high-heeled shoes. I had a few occasions before the accident when I put on my dress and heels, and I really liked the feeling. I felt like the most beautiful and elegant girl in the world, and I could hardly wait for the eighth-grade prom. It never crossed my mind that I would experience it from such a position. I thought I would be on the dance floor too, feeling good with my other classmates graduating from the eighth grade. Although I was with my class, I was stuck at a table, in a chair, from where I watched them, destroyed and helpless as they had fun.

The day after the prom I went to Bucharest with my mother, father and uncle. We asked my uncle to take us because not even half of our luggage would fit in our car. The hotel we booked was not at all like we had seen in the pictures. I couldn't even get through the door with the wheelchair, so we had to look for a hotel near the airport that would have wheelchair access. We stayed at Rin, and at four in the morning we woke up and prepared to leave.

I was very emotional as I had put all my hopes in the German clinic and I was expecting to return with great results. I said goodbye to my father and uncle, and set off with my mother on a new journey. The flight was pleasant and in just two hours we arrived in Stuttgart. From there we were picked up in a car adapted for the wheelchair (it was something I had never seen in my country) and taken to Ulm, to the recovery clinic. I didn't speak English very well, and so to ensure an effective communication regarding the hospitalisation and the recovery programme, my aunt, my mother's sister, and her daughter, who had been living in Germany for many years, came from a few hundred kilometres away. They arrived the same day as we did and stayed with us for about three days. Their presence was extremely helpful because we were able to find out all the details that we needed to know.

It was a very large hospital, but the wards did not look worth 700 euros a day. I had no refrigerator or TV in the room. To be fair, everything was adapted for people with disabilities. The first days were hard while we learned about the programme, then we got used to it. The only downside was the food. The food was not nice, we only touched the breakfast. Lunch and dinner were made up of cream soups, asparagus and some strange stuff that our taste buds didn't agree with. We bought some food from the clinic store, until we became friends with the medical nurses and found food leaflets from different restaurants and fast food places, and sometimes we ordered from there.

Apart from the food, I really liked the centre's openness and way of thinking. I liked that they found solutions for every issue and were very orderly and disciplined. There was a big difference between the hospitals in Romania and the hospital in Ulm. In Ulm, the medical staff did my hygiene, washed me, drained my urine and dressed me. They also transferred me from bed to chair and back again. I had a fixed time for everything. My mother helped them, of course, but in Romania she has been doing most of this alone.

'Your wheel chair is for older people, and you are a wonderful young woman. We need to make a change,' the medical nurses told me the first morning of the hospitalisation.

They put me in a new, electric chair. It was adapted to my condition. They fixed me in with Velcro to hold my torso and keep me balanced and taught me to use it. Even though I couldn't use my fingers, they adjusted the joystick so that I could operate it with my right wrist. This gave me my first bit of independence. I roamed around the hospital all day. It felt like I walked alone, not on my feet, but on wheels. For me it was progress. I no longer depended on anyone to push my chair. After the success of using the phone, using the chair was the second thing I could do on my own.

They also brought me some adapted devices to help me eat on my own, but I couldn't manage them too well. I could only use them on top of a table, but even so it was difficult for me. I had started the recovery programme and was feeling hopeful. However, after two weeks I found out that it was not all as I had expected. The Germans were well organised but they were so slow! They always chose the easiest option so they didn't have to work too hard. The Romanian therapists, at least those at the Robănescu Hospital in the capital, were a hundred times more hardworking, engaged and dedicated in what they did. The Germans had many more extraordinarily advanced devices, which the Romanians only dreamed of, but they only used them on patients who were easy to work with, that is, those patients who had a high degree of mobility. Obviously, this did not include me. I begged the therapists who worked with me to put me in the exoskeleton, but they told me it was too complicated and they didn't even bother to try. The exoskeleton is like a robot which mimics walking and it can walk you all over the place, even outside the therapy room. I saw lots of patients using it, moving through the huge hospital garden and I was very sorry that I could not do it.

The Germans were good in terms of hydrotherapy. They had an adapted pool for people in wheelchairs. In Romania, it all comes down to tough physical work, the therapist and the carer destroying their backs by lifting patients up stairs, onto the physiotherapy tables, wherever and whenever it is needed. Here, devices replaced human work, which was much easier. Sadly, they only took me to hydrotherapy once, stating that my urinary tract infection could not be treated and I could contaminate the water and affect the other patients – even though my bladder was drained before being put in the pool. They told me that if I wanted to continue the hydrotherapy, I should have a catheter put in my bellybutton, which would replace the urethral catheterisation, and so get rid of the urinary tract infection.

'Have you thought about it? What is the final decision regarding the bellybutton tube?' one of the therapists asked me.

'I'm not going to do it. The nurses showed me some patients who have that tube and I didn't like what I saw at all. They had a urine bag attached to their feet hooked up to an umbilical cord. I do not accept such a treatment. The urine drainage that I am doing now is the best option, I have no tube or bag in sight and no other permanent tube through my body.'

I was more and more disappointed because the therapies I was following were few and I didn't feel any improvement. In the email conversations, they boasted a lot about their services, but the reality was not even half what they had presented in writing. We asked for an early discharge because it was a waste of money but we had to wait anyway for a week for some papers.

On the final weekend we went to Kaufland supermarket by bus. The store was ten kilometres away from the hospital and I was amazed by the infrastructure I saw as we travelled. The bus had a wheelchair ramp, and when the driver saw us, he got off to come to help my mother. Each sidewalk had a ramp to climb or descend, and people looked at me normally, not grimacing or frowning when they saw me. It was, indeed, an educated country in every way.

I tried to buy an electric chair, like the one they used with me during my stay in the clinic. I did not want to return to the old chair which I could not move. The hospital owned a store for medical equipment and I found a wheel chair for 2,300 euros. It was a second-hand chair, one of the cheapest. A new one with more facilities was worth 10,000 euros, but I was satisfied with it because I felt that it was all I needed at that moment. The cost of the chair was covered by the Always Close Foundation, and because I did not stay in Germany for the entire period, the remaining money was returned to the foundation's account and was used later to help me, covering some of the recovery therapies and dozens of medical devices I needed.

Before we left, the head of the department wanted to talk to us to understand why we had asked for an early discharge. We took part in a kind of meeting with the head of the department and the therapists who took care of me. Another therapist, who was Romanian (there were many Romanians in that hospital), assisted to make sure both sides in the conversation fully understood each other. Everyone spoke English in that room, but the presence of the Romanian helped me express myself, because I didn't know all the terms. We started to tell them our complaints, meaning mine, and to highlight how their promises in the emails did not match the reality. After listening to us, the doctor replied.

'You can look anywhere in this world, but you will not find treatment that will make you walk or feel anything from the chest down. You already move too much given the severity of your trauma. Most of our cases in a similar situation to you only move their heads. The fact that you have motor signs on your upper limbs is more than the maximum you could achieve.'

Although many had tried to convey this truth to me in more subtle and gentle words, I did not believe them, but the German had something special that made him very solemn when he spoke. I don't know what I answered or if I was still rational in those moments. I felt a shiver through my whole body, and I wanted to disappear from that room. My soul ached and I felt blood flowing out from my heart. I felt like I couldn't face the reality anymore, but my brain turned out to be stronger and it seemed to mock me with its resilience.

For more than a year, I had lived with the hope and purpose that the day would come when my life would return to normal. At that moment, the words of the German doctor hit me in the middle of my head, shook me from all sides and woke me up to reality. More than ever, I realised what a slap in the face my life had given me. A slap that not only knocked me down from all points of view, but made me want nothing more than the moment when my heart would stop beating. I was a helpless person defeated by a too cruel destiny, from which I had no way out. I realised that that damn accident had stolen everything from me, and that the fact that I had survived had no other purpose than to dry my soul, for I had lost my body on that morning when the Universe laughed in my face and played a checkmate. I realised that I would never be able to feel and control my body again, to dance, to return to people and to lead a normal life. I realised that my whole life would be as it was last year, that I would never have another moment of happiness, and my soul would remain the prisoner of a lifeless body. Those important stages in everyone's life were going on in my mind, and I understood that I had no way to live them. Adolescence, high school, college, the moment I fell in love were just a few of the sequences that went through my head, and I knew I would never know them. I understood that I would remain just a person who causes pain, suffering and torment. I was exhausted, mentally exhausted, and I had no power or will left.

38

A different person

I went through moments of living nightmare; through moments that showed me how much suffering, pain, hatred, humiliation and indifference there is in this great world. I went through situations that made me an inert person, someone who could no longer react in any way to pain. I shed millions of tears that took my breath away. I lay between four walls for hundreds of days, and loneliness was my only friend. I blamed and hated myself because to some extent I had caused my suffering on my own.

I was a completely changed person. My face didn't look like what it once was. I rarely looked at myself in the mirror, and when I did I wanted to disappear off the face of the Earth. Everyone had forgotten me, I only had my parents. Mara and some relatives sometimes visited me, but their presence disturbed me. To hear that others were living beautiful, untroubled lives hurt me terribly. To hear Mara tell me about the boy she fell in love with stung me from the inside. I was like a person preparing to take their last breath. This misfortune had given me only two options: to agonise continuously until I would probably have to go to a mental institution, where I would find my end, or to fight with what I had left. Practically nothing or almost nothing. Only my brain was entirely good.

I agonised until 2017, when I chose to invest in myself and try to do something with my existence. I understood that I was

the only person who could help myself and I chose, with the
support of my parents, to start stitching my mental wounds. Up
until then, even though my morale was down, I did not neglect
school and continued home schooling. In the ninth grade, as
promised by the inspectorate, they put me in a high school that
still had places, and considered my preference for natural sciences.
Although the high school was of a mediocre level, this was because
of the indolent students and their low results. The teachers I
had exceeded my expectations and saw me as a normal student,
looking beyond the wheelchair. I only had a small incident with
the Romanian teacher, not related to my problem, but to the
teaching method, and the high school principal proved to be
very open and understanding, and as soon as he heard what it
was about he changed my teacher. Some colleagues were curious
to meet me and came to my house to exchange a few words.
I finished the ninth grade with an average score of over 9.70,
which allowed me to transfer, also to the natural sciences, back to
Alecsandri College, where I had been in high school. I felt that I
was back in the right place.

At Alecsandri College I came across an exceptional class
teacher. He had a modern style, with parties and trips in his
blood, a teacher any high school student would want. Mr Puiu
teaches mathematics and at first sight you would perceive him
as being extremely severe. However, he proved to be the coolest
class teacher ever. I didn't really participate in all the wonderful
moments that my colleagues enjoyed, but from all the actions
that they carried out, I realised what a great person the class
teacher was. My colleagues were also a cool group. Even though
I had never met them all, they looked like teenagers who were
connected to each other. I didn't have expectations from them
because I knew what the result would be. I knew they wouldn't
pay much attention to me and that's why I didn't insist on boring

them. The class teacher always visited me together with two or three, sometimes even four, classmates for the math class. That way I could exchange a few words with them. But it was nothing more. They didn't try to help me in any way, to take me out or to visit me more often, they only came with the teacher. Mara was still the only person who called and visited me.

When a high school is ranked at the top, you have the expectation that all the people there, especially the teachers, will be excellent academically. You also expect good moral principles and a human approach. In reality, things are different. I came across two teachers who put me down and destroyed my mental state even more. One taught biology, my favourite subject, and the other chemistry.

'I waste too much time coming to your home to teach you. During this time, I could prepare students for the Biology Olympics. They are my priority and this is what I do, home-schooling is not for me. I only do 'excellency' with my students,' the biology teacher told me in our first class.

Her words hit me in the head. Though I had understood the words of the German doctor because they expressed a cruel reality that could not be changed, I could not understand the teacher. Somehow, she was telling me that I was wasting her time and that I didn't deserve her attention. Her words humiliated me and reminded me, once again, how unimportant I am to society.

The chemistry teacher did not say anything to me directly, but she took care to complain to the high school principal saying that she should have counselling before she taught me. I didn't bark, I did nothing to scare her, I was just a person in a wheelchair in front of them. A person with a major physical deficit. My brain was untouched. I could think, talk, and express myself as other people considered normal but she treated me like an object. I didn't understand where the need for counselling came from. The

principal was slow to act and took a whole semester to change
these two ladies and send me other teachers. During which time,
I didn't do chemistry at all and I was left with only those notions
that the teacher taught me in the only two hours she came to me.
In biology I saw the teacher face to face about five times, which
was not enough to teach me, to listen to me, to give me tests and
to mark my knowledge. In chemistry, nothing mattered, neither
the grades nor the tests, because the lady did what she wanted.

It's cruel to behave like that with a student who is already
carrying a heavy burden on their shoulders. Even worse is
that those ladies have children, whom they certainly educated
according to the same poor principles. Worse still is that before
I gave my thesis in biology, the teacher spoke badly about me
and my parents during a class which Mara was in. She told the
students that we were a madhouse and that there were cockroaches
crawling across our apartment. We didn't have a villa with a pool
or the conditions of the lady at home, but we really didn't have
cockroaches in the flat. My parents were exemplary people. My
mother was a perfect housewife and a woman who always put
everything in order, and my father a model man. Despite the
many problems we had, my mother always found time to clean
the flat, even if she had to stay up until two a.m. so everything
was spotless. Our apartment was very small and cramped and had
no state-of-the-art furniture, but it was always clean and tidy.

I am overwhelmed when I see people like this. People who
have no idea what suffering is and live in a crystal ball, being
protected from the evil that surrounds them. People who defy
others through their behaviour. No matter how rich they are, they
want even more and are never satisfied with what they have, nor
are they grateful for the happy life God has given them. Of course,
many have worked for what they have achieved, but it is not fair
to throw stones at less fortunate people. It's not fair to make fun

of those who don't have a different outfit for every day. It's not fair to marginalise someone based on the way they look without considering what skills they have. It is inhuman to destroy the hopes of a student eager to learn, and it is inappropriate when you have a certain status and are expected to behave in a certain way but in reality, you do not care for anybody's feelings.

It seemed that every time I tried to find my balance, a situation came up that dragged me down. Every time I had the feeling that I was up, I blinked and the next second I was down, but I never gave up. I kept getting up whenever I got hit. I kept hoping that eventually life would get bored and stop striking me, but it wasn't going to be like that. In May 2017, I was in a recovery centre in Techirghiol, accompanied by both parents. During my transfer to the table intended for physiotherapy, my mother got a sudden severe back pain. For a good few days she barely moved and was left with a lot of pain, but also sensitivity on her right leg. In the first hours after the incident she could not even get out of bed. The situation was so serious that my father had to help her urinate in a bed pan. I was in one bed completely immobilised, and my mother in another could barely turn to one side. My first base person had fallen. My father knew how to drain my urine, to change me and so on, because he had to learn everything back in December 2016, when my mother was away from home for appendicitis surgery and septal deviation, but he was clumsier than my mother, he didn't have her dexterity and he didn't know all the little important things. In such moments you are either finished or survive and rise even stronger.

Because I had been lying in a bed for a very long time and I didn't pay attention to my diet anymore, I put on a lot of weight. My parents could barely lift me. To see them sad, crying, and tormented was hard to bear. I had given up telling them that I could no longer stand my life and I was trying to come to their

aid. So I had to struggle a lot to lose weight. The extra pounds
had become a burden for me too, not just for my parents' backs.
I couldn't find clothes to fit me anymore. In the winter and cold
season, I needed a waist-length jacket that was easy enough for
my parents to dress me. I searched dozens of stores but couldn't
find one. When I was in Alba Iulia, in the centre where I had
to travel a distance of 750–800 meters between therapy and
accommodation, and it was snowing outside, I had to be dressed
in several layers so my body didn't freeze. I couldn't feel anything
from the chest down anyway, but my body was very sensitive
and any cut was very difficult to heal. For more than half a year I
tested different diets and programs given by nutritionists, doctors
and fitness trainers, but I failed to lose much weight. I tried
smoothies, soy milk, frozen fruit, turkey breast, shrimp, seeds and
everything I was prescribed, but without much success. That was
until I came across the Rina diet.

The Rina diet is designed around having a different food group
every day and it seemed to me the easiest to follow compared
to everything I had tried until then, except for the water day.
For the first four days I ate a different food group. On the first
day protein, on the second starch, On the third any type of
carbohydrate and on the fourth fruits then I started again with
protein and so on for three months. You could eat vegetables every
day. After three months I had to go on with "maintenance" and
continued for another three months in which I could mix the
food, but not at the same meal (protein at lunch and carbs in the
evening). Breakfast consisted only of fruits or vegetables, and once
a month I had to drink only water without eating anything that
day.

'Make me understand! So you're saying you'll lose weight by
eating cakes and pasta?' said Silviu, the physiotherapist visiting me
at home, laughing one afternoon as he mobilised my lower limbs.

'And potatoes,' added my mother giggling.

'Yes. What's so hard to understand? I've read the comments of people who got results,' I replied. 'One day I eat grilled meat, another day baked potatoes, another pretzels at lunch and in the evening cake and dark chocolate, and the fourth day I eat only fruit.'

'Aha, well, Andreea,' Silviu replied, continuing to laugh, accompanied by my mother.

'You laugh, but you will see how slender I'll be. And it's really easy to follow this diet,' I said seriously.

Oh, it really wasn't easy at all! At first I had moments of doubt and I wanted to give up, believing that I would never be able to lose weight because not being able to move I could not burn the calories. I couldn't even follow my progress with the scales. The only opportunity I had to weigh myself was at the recovery centre in Bucharest, on a special chair. However, I measured my progress by clothes. In three months I had lost enough weight to fit my clothes from before the accident. I was so relieved. I also kept to the maintenance period, then for four months I ate everything I wanted, in moderation of course. I resumed the diet the following year because I had put some of the weight back on again. It was even harder for me the second time because I was in the second semester of the eleventh grade, during the trial baccalaureate exams. I was also preparing for admission to medical school. Learning all the cranial nerves with their origins during the water day was not great, but I managed to motivate myself and I lost the kilos.

39

Paving for the future

I had wanted to study medicine since the fifth grade, right from my first lessons in biology. Even though we were studying plant structure that year, I discovered several segments of the human body in the lab which aroused my curiosity. I was fascinated by the way we are made up and function. I continued to read various articles about the human body and as I progressed I came to know clearly that in high school I wanted to study natural sciences, and later to apply to medical school and become a doctor. I knew that the job involved a lot of training, dedication and empathy, but I wanted to help, to contribute to human happiness, and I wanted to do good for those in need.

The car accident had not only taken away my physical independence, but also all my dreams. I was living in fear, confined within closed horizons and never sure of what the next second might bring. I didn't know what was coming. Due to my physical situation, my future was uncertain, almost non-existent. Even though I had found my inner strength and was ready to face the challenges, reality always reminded me that it was above all my wishes. However, I took strength from the stories of others, people with similar cases to mine who became doctors, and I thought that if they could do this, then I too would surely succeed. In addition to Dr Onose, whom I met a month after the accident, I had also heard of three other people in wheelchairs in Romania (there are a lot more abroad) who graduated from medical school and became doctors. However, their cases were different from mine. Dr Onose was already a doctor, when bad luck nailed him in a wheelchair, and in two of the three cases I had read about it was said that they were already medical students when the tragedy happened to them. They had less trouble with admissions process and systematic prejudice, even though some considered their re-entry into the field inappropriate. In the third case, the young woman had suffered from muscular dystrophy since birth and used a wheelchair; she was nevertheless admitted. However, in all of the cases that I learned about, those concerned enjoyed much greater independence than I, and there was only one of them whose condition was really comparable to my own.

Of course, medicine is not just about surgery and A&E. Medicine also has branches that involve less physical effort, such as radiology, psychiatry and laboratory medicine. I determinded that this was the path I would take. The exam consisted of biology (eleventh grade) and chemistry (tenth and eleventh grade). I needed a teacher, especially in chemistry, to train me. I searched for half a year and just when I wanted to give up, a life-saver appeared. Most teachers refused when they heard I was in a wheelchair, and others didn't do home classes. Eventually, I found Mrs Solomon, who was retired but was filling in for a colleague. Even at the age of sixty-six, she knew every concentration and reaction and formula. The woman also knew what suffering meant, because she was caring for her husband, who had suffered a stroke about seven years ago. The thing is that, in the end, help comes from people who have had difficulties in life.

Home schooling in Romania is organised in the worst possible way. There is only one pot for all cases. I, who had a normal intellect, was considered to be on the same level as those who suffer from severe learning disabilities or debilitating mental illnesses. This meant that instead of getting the same number of hours as my peers, I was only allocated fifty minutes a week per subject. My classmates at school had at least triple that, not to mention the overtime that the teachers did with them. Given that I had to take the same, equally-difficult exams as my peers who had benefited from more teaching hours than me, this did not seem very fair. Of course, I was upset in vain, because I had no one to argue with, and even if I asked anything, the articles of the law were thrown at me, fluttered around my nose, and everyone shrugged.

Most of the teachers visited me only for the hours they were paid for, because as the Romanian saying goes, "You can be my brother, but the cheese is for money". It didn't matter that in the short time we had, I couldn't cover all the subjects. If I wanted more, it was my problem. However, there were also some exceptions. For the Romanian language classes, in my final years, I was lucky to be taught by someone who was not only a super teacher, but also a super person.

She was always interested in the quality of whatever she was doing. Although the programme provided for only one-and-a-half hours a week, she would stay for three and even four hours, especially in the twelfth grade. All the information she taught in the class she taught me too. It was obvious that she was a person who exercised her profession with pleasure and passion. Romanian teachers rarely make you understand and explain every little thing in a literary text. My teacher was so good that even "Luceafărul" (a famous long Romanian poem) was explained to me from cover to cover. She read me every verse and not a word remained unexplained.

The mathematics teacher (who was the class teacher too) also spent more time with me, but not in the way the Romanian literature teacher did. We spent more time talking with him and the classmates who accompanied him. He never understood how hard it was for me to learn maths. Because I couldn't move my fingers I couldn't hold the pen in my hand. Maths is a subject that is learned by practising and writing on paper. I had to learn everything orally. I had to take private tuition in maths from the tenth grade because it was not enough for me to do the five or six exercises per week with the class teacher. It was simple for him. He would come, teach me my new lesson, solve some exercises and give me a sheet with 100 exercises as homework. The next week we would either work on two or three more exercises from the last lesson or continue with a new one. In three years he never checked my homework, but I did it every time. In fact, I worked on it with Mrs Ani, a teacher and a person who will remain forever in my soul. For Mrs Ani and the Romanian literature teacher, I would repeat high school a few more times. I'm not saying the class teacher was a bad teacher. On the contrary. He was highly professional, and I appreciated his teaching. I'm just saying that he had taken the time to get to know me and put himself in my shoes, maybe he would have handled things differently.

I didn't have much contact with the other teachers. They came, did their job then left.

40

Ultimate bad luck?

My needs grew from year to year. This meant that expenses were also increasing. Medical supplies were very expensive. Sadly, I got a bad pressure sore, which affected me for more than two years. A single dressing cost between twenty-five and thirty lei. A set of ten foils soaked in specific treatment was 250 lei. Some months we spent 5,000 lei, just for my care, not counting the expenses that piled up during periods of hospitalisation. People with big hearts were still helping us. Looking through the comments of a fundraising event, I saw one which said, "This girl will surely get good money from insurance, maybe even millions of euros, considering how badly she was damaged."

This girl, meaning myself, had the "ultimate bad luck", as a lawyer would say, because the car was insured with Astra – a company that went bankrupt in the year of the accident. Basically, through the open court, we tried to obtain a little so I could at least buy some diapers. The first trial lasted about two years. I attended one hearing myself. Alex was there too. He walked past me, but he didn't say "Hello." I was a little outraged at the time and I was thinking "Dude, you idiot, you almost killed me, you screwed me up for life, and you don't say anything?" But another voice was fighting with the first, saying "And who made you get in the car with him? It was your choice, take it and live with it!"

The first trial resulted in a lamentable verdict. I was compensated with a miserable amount, which did not even cover the cost of hospitalisation for the three weeks I stayed in Germany. I think the judge thought it was child's play, and that I had suffered a little scratch. Otherwise I can't explain it. You don't have to have graduated from Oxford to understand words that are clear for everyone: "complete loss of muscle function and total motor deficit". It is easy to understand what such a prognosis means. Paralysis involves a social life equal to zero, the inability to work or to start a family, and the need for supervision and constant care provided by another person, sometimes two. Those caring for a patient also become indirect victims because their health deteriorates faster due to the manoeuvres used for care. And the knock-on effects can continue. Romania's justice is pathetic, and most judges are very superficial. The compensation was only charged to Astra (the vehicle insurance company), and not to Alex, as if I had caused the accident.

I challenged the decision and changed lawyers. Dozens of "rejects the appeal as unfounded" followed. Alex's lawyer was not utterly insensitive, but his attitude left me speechless. Good. I understand that the wind is blowing through your conscience. I understand not to interfere. Not to care for ruining my life. Do nothing to help me. But to deny that my parents are injured parties and to say that the claim is unfounded is totally immoral, inhuman. How can you argue that my parents were not affected? My mother has two herniated discs from lifting me and she had to give up her job to care for me and wipe my ass every day. She gave up her personal life for me. My father has spine problems, and some other issues. They both have hypertension. They are physically and mentally exhausted. From one day to the next, their condition deteriorates, and you, the defendant's lawyer, comes and says that the parents have suffered nothing.

I understand that you are supposed to defend your client, who suffered no injury, but obstructing me is too much. I sometimes wonder if such people are not afraid of God's wrath. Aren't they afraid that God will strike them down and blow them away?

This is not about getting rich. All the money in this world can't restore my life as it was before the accident. This is about survival. The fact that my survival costs hundreds of lei every day. What will happen to me when my family can't cope anymore? Did the judge consider this when coming to his decision? Nobody comes to care for me unpaid. These things, but also many others, do not seem to have been understood by any judge. After several trials, the decision was a better one than the first, but not satisfactory and not even useful. The sums were supposed to be covered by the same useless "dead body". Of course, Astra's representatives were acquitted because of the bankruptcy law. Behind them, and any bankrupt insurance company, is the Guarantee Fund. They set a fixed amount regardless of the court decision, this being the only compensation I could get. The rest of the money is to be compensated when the "dead body resurrects", meaning never. In cases similar to mine but where the insurance company had not gone bankrupt, a monthly social benefit was given, and parents were also compensated. Even if these sums could not bring smiles or happiness to those who received them, they did provide a drop of freedom and guaranteed the safety of tomorrow.

Only when you hit a boulder do you really understand that your wounds cannot be sewn up with money. You understand that health cannot be replaced by material things. You understand that in most cases your current state of health is irreversible. But, in extreme situations, money is what keeps you afloat and facilitates your independence.

41

After a while

My eighteenth birthday celebration was not an ordinary one. It was not as I dreamed it would be when I was younger. I didn't have those dancing moments with my parents. I didn't even dance with my friends. I just sat at a table and looked at the others. But I wasn't sad. I was regretful and it hurt that I wasn't like the others, but I was happy because I didn't spend the celebration alone. I was surrounded by about thirty people, relatives and friends. Of course, I didn't mean much to most of them, but the fact that they were present and surrounded me that day mattered to me a lot. I have missed many situations, emotions and events in the years since the accident. I have especially missed people. People to call me; to support me; to involve me in their lives. People who understand that although I have lost many abilities, I am still here and I am not just a non-entity.

The next year after my eighteenth birthday celebration, in 2019, I managed to reclaim myself, the person, someone who has a whole life ahead. I understood that will, ambition and action can make the impossible possible. I still suffer from the same major physical deficits as before, but even though I can only use my right arm, and not even all of it, I have not stopped working to achieve certain goals. The loneliness I knew and thousands of barriers that society put against me did not bring me down, but made me stronger. They tested my limits and made me the person I am today.

Over time, I have learned that I do not need great things to feel fulfilled. I have also learned that happiness lies behind what I have, not what I lack. Even though so much was taken from me, I have learned that what I have left is all that ever mattered. I'm not saying that I'm one hundered per cent happy with my life, but I say that it's important to be satisfied with what we have and to capitalise on that little something. This is how we will find out how lucky we are, compared to others who don't even have as much or don't realise that they can do even more.

Although I have had more failures than accomplishments, I have never stopped striving to realise my goals. And that's because success lies in the power to not give up on your dream. Failures are said to provide the fuel for the greatest achievements and successes in life. To this I would add that the harshest words addressed to a "small" person can build strength in that person. However, there is a difference between words that convey an unbearable reality to the recipient and words that are said out of carelessness, ignorance or malice. Well, I managed, to some extent, to get over the words of the doctors who told me that I would never walk again, because they didn't do anything wrong when they informed me about this reality. This is, nonetheless, a reality that will surely change in a few years because medicine has always shown that it is constantly improving. It was the times when I was told, "I'm wasting too much time coming to teach you. I only train the Olympians", "I have to go to a psychologist before I come to you", "The ramp costs too much and we can't buy it. And the carpenter can't make one", and many similar things, It was at these times when I felt worse than when I was told I would never walk. And this is because there is a huge difference between situations that cannot be achieved because it really is impossible and those that can be achieved, but there is no will to do so. It's just that not all people have the will. However, it is within our power to have a positive influence on society and change the mind-set. And all this happens through people. Dedicated people.

People for whom happiness means the happiness of another. People who do not give up no matter how hard it may be and reach the top of the mountain no matter how many obstacles they encounter. People who cross the sea no matter how many storms arise along the way.

It is also in our power to be valuable people. Let's not only worry about success, fame and money. Let us concern ourselves, first, with our soul. Through my tragic experience, I also learned that beauty, wealth and success are ephemeral, things that are lost in time. Our value is defined by what we are inside and how we act.

In March 2019, I became a model at the Atypic Beauty event, an event held in several major cities across the country, featuring twelve models in wheelchairs and twelve local celebrities. Atypic Beauty models are people who have either ended up in wheelchairs due to unfortunate events or who were born with a physical disability. However, despite their disability, they have managed to acquire a status and to integrate or reintegrate into society, thus they can be a positive influence on society through their actions. The girls and boys taking part in the event are real role models, people who have managed to work and be successful in various fields. The concept is unique in Romania and extremely exciting.

Magda Coman founded the association in 2013 and is the event creator. She ended up in a wheelchair more than ten years ago, at a time when she was a catwalk model, and worked in fashion shows for various Romanian designers. After her life changed, she was ambitious and became the only Romanian model in a wheelchair who managed to practice internationally. Atypic Beauty was born from Magda's desire to change, through refinement and elegance, the attitude of Romanian society towards people with disabilities, and to highlight their successes. Each edition has behind it an army of people who help to ensure the event runs smoothly. The annual galas take place at the Palace of the Parliament, and are presented by Andreea Marin (a famous former TV hostess).

Becoming a model for these events helped me a lot. It increased my self-esteem and helped me to rebuild a positive relationship with myself, and for that I can only be grateful to Magda and thank her. I came to understand that I had to appreciate myself more and continue to fight so as to look forward to the future.

Between us, the models, a beautiful friendship has been growing, especially with Magda, the person who inspired us. For me it was hard at first. In my life there had been another person with the same name, a person who is linked to my condition, and that made it harder for me to get used to the current Magda. Whenever I said "I have to write to Magda ...", "Magda said that", "Magda is waiting for us at..." and so on, my thoughts flew to someone else. It is a psychological threshold that has been difficult to overcome, but I have learned to live with it.

42

Five years on

For me, March is an overwhelming month. So overwhelming that sometimes I want it to disappear from the calendar. A few days before the fifth anniversary of the accident, I wrote a post on Facebook. After almost five years I was publicly opening up about my life; me, who a few years before did not even want to be seen, let alone photographed. I wrote:

In a few days it will be 5 years ...

5 years since the event that turned my life upside down;

5 years since the accident that stole my independence and made me a prisoner of an object, a wheelchair;

5 years since my body stopped listening to me;

5 years since I discovered how much drama, suffering, malice, hatred, wickedness and humiliation exist in this world.

Although almost 5 years have passed, I feel everything so close, so fresh, as if everything happened 5 minutes ago. I see, feel, hear and smell all the critical moments I went through even now, after 5 years.

I see the door of the ICU where at least one person a day came out covered with a white sheet from toe to head, accompanied by two nurses. The person, most likely, passed away sad and upset because they didn't have time to say goodbye to their loved ones. Many stories entered that door every day, stories that maybe ended then, but also others, which continue today. Beyond that door were my parents, who stayed there from morning until late in the evening, waiting for news from doctors and for visiting hours so they could stay with me.

The amalgam of pain was something I had never felt before, along with fear and despair, increasing with each passing day, and I still don't know what pressed me hardest: the physical pain, the fear that I couldn't breathe properly even with the oxygen mask, or my despair in being only able to move my eyes.

I still hear the sound of the equipment that monitored my heart activity, and the whistling sound that came from other patients when the wave from the EKG went flat forever.

The smell of the IVs, serums, blood, wounds and bandages that I encountered daily, each hour, I still feel even now, and I could distinguish them even blindfolded.

"You can look anywhere in this world, but you will not find a treatment that will make you walk or ever feel anything from the chest down." These were the words of a German doctor that I heard a year after the accident, words that I had heard from others, in a subtler form. Words with weight, with too much weight, but real.

More than a year and a half had passed, during which time I had been hoping and waiting for the physical injuries to heal, but this was not the case. Only the surface wounds healed, leaving the scars, but the physical wounds on the inside remained. Then I understood that a spinal cord injury does not heal because medicine has no solution for it.

The days went by, but my physical and mental suffering remained. Slowly, slowly, with the support of my parents, I began to patch my mental wounds on my own. I chose to better myself and build something. I understood that if I didn't do something to save myself, no one would be able to do it for me. I understood that when it's hard, I shouldn't give up, expecting to feel better later. I understood that the millions of tears I shed would not reverse time or heal me. There are moments when I feel as if the sky has fallen on my head, but then it's as if I see myself in front of me, standing up, asking myself, "Come on, is this all you can do?" and then I gather all my strength and I realise that I can do more again!

I chose to see the good side of things. I chose to thank God that I got away with these injuries, because yes, it could be even worse. I chose to enjoy the fact that I can see, hear, talk, interact; I have memories, I have close parents who love me unconditionally and support me; I chose to enjoy the fact that I EXIST.

I chose to overcome all the humiliations and barriers that society offers me every day, because I had the misfortune to be born in a country where to fight the system and the humiliation you are forced to endure is more terrible than the disease/trauma you are already struggling with. I love my country and I would not leave because we, the people, are the ones who made it sick and we too have to treat it.

For change to take place, I understood that I, you, all of us must be the ones who undergo transformations. We have

reached a level where we forget who we really are and put first
the professions acquired in time, such as doctor, lawyer, teacher,
bricklayer, cook, etc., forgetting our primary profession: that of
being a human being. We forget that at birth we each received
from God this gift, this primary profession and we practically
make fun of what God created.

We end up dehumanising ourselves in the face of well-being,
and when something bad happens to someone around us and
no longer meets all the "standards", we move away and continue
our life according to the principle "God forbid, it's a good that
hasn't happened to me!" We forget to help our neighbour and
to contribute to making our society a unitary whole. When
we gain status, we forget where we came from and we want to
eliminate those who, we believe, are inferior to us. We run away
from responsibilities and do not admit our failures. We end up
forgetting those who once fed us, we are individualistic and we
are ashamed to admit when we are wrong. We do not want to
apologise for fear of being degraded.

We, the society, are the problem, not the country. Our country
is perfect, it has a wonderful landscape and multiple resources that
we can use, but it doesn't have good leaders, able to make wise
investments in health, education, highways, to implement fair
and dignified laws, to capitalise on it and make it shine. We do
not want to communicate and do everything as a team because we
want praise only for ourselves. We do not want to be open to the
suggestions of others, and when someone different appears, from
any point of view, we try to shut them out using as many padlocks
as possible and build walls to try to eliminate them as soon as
possible, in an attempt to make them give up. We put the outer
beauty, which is ephemeral, first, and we judge by the packaging,
without having the patience to explore the contents.

In this way we make our country laughable and promote baseness and cowardice. Taking responsibility is the first change we need to make. Indeed, taking responsibility is difficult, but doing so also bolsters our courage and makes us better able to face the consequences of our decisions and actions. That's what GREAT PEOPLE do. It is in our power to live our lives with dignity and to transform preconceived ideas into positive beliefs.

I do not want to emphasise the drama I've been through, to generalise or offend, but I want to emphasise a reality. A reality that many of us face every day. In the last five years, seventy per cent of the people I met and knew were exactly as I described above, and only thirty per cent were people from whom I could never have expected it, but who made a real difference, which meant much more, though they were fewer. Seemingly simple people, but rich in soul, who turned out to be people in the true sense of the word. People who do not even have enough for themselves, but whose soul is turned upside down when they notice the need in the eyes of another. People who share their little with those around them, people who deserve all of our respect. People who enjoy the happiness of others and for whom well-being is not defined by something physical, but by something that comes from within, from the soul.

Let's open our eyes and put aside pride and selfishness, stop thinking only about ourselves and our needs, and at least try to do good on a random day.

"Be human, it's free!"

By that statement I wanted to raise awareness, understanding and responsibility. It is important to analyse ourselves. Let's find out who and what we are. Let's identify our mistakes and correct them in time. And the most important thing is to give ourselves time and patience.

In the first years after the accident, I hated the word "patience". I had moments when I thought that if I heard it once more I'd go crazy. Some said it only as a formality because that's what they say when you go through a difficult period – "be patient, it will be fine". But others knew what they were saying because they spoke from experience. It was hard for me to learn to live with suffering. To survive. For I will never be able to get over it. There is an open wound in my soul that will never heal. Patience helped me reinvent myself. Patience has created opportunities for me to continue to survive. Time does not heal wounds at all. Time only deepens them. But it depends on us and our choices. It is our choice whether we choose to deepen our wounds even more or chose instead to patch them up with our hope, as one dresses a wound. Even if we know that they will never be healed, what is around them will come to life. It is a huge satisfaction to know that you live not only to consume, but that you have a purpose, one that always keeps you active and makes you want to wake up the next morning.

43

Life does not stop

Both the festive class and the prom took place. Unfortunately, I could not feel the same emotions as my peers. For me, high school was a period during which I accumulated more knowledge and that's it. I haven't been on any trips; didn't attend any parties; couldn't take part in other activities. I didn't have much fun. But I had classes every day and I was glad that someone was crossing the threshold of my house. I interacted more with teachers than with students.

In the first semester I went to the biology and maths classes in the high school, thinking that this would help me with the baccalaureate exam. But I gave up quickly. The high school principal didn't want to buy a ramp because it was too expensive. However, I do not think that a piece of wood or some cement could be considered of greater worth than a person's health and wellbeing. There was no ground floor. All the classrooms were at basement level or on the first floor, so inevitably there were a lot of stairs. There were also spiral staircases to navigate, as well as steps at the front entrance. We drove into the yard. I had the class in the basement. A few students carried my chair, which weighed no less than eighty kilograms, and my father and another classmate carried me in their arms tens of metres to the chair. It was not worth the effort. I learned the same material I could learn at home. During the class breaks, I barely talked to anyone, as most of my classmates went outside. Mara was the only one who stayed with me. So I gave up.

On the day of graduation, I joined my classmates for the parade, which made me feel good. I would have regretted it if I hadn't gone, even if I wasn't as excited as the others. I felt excluded from many of the activities. I don't appear in any pictures dressed in my graduation cloak. I wasn't even on stage, when all the graduates shouted; I couldn't go up there. I couldn't throw my cap in the air. Many things were not for me as they were for others. The banquet was not too different either. Seeing over 300 young people my age jumping up and down was not very pleasant. Watching the girls in the arms of the boys on the dance floor was overwhelming. I was jealous and it hurt a lot. All this because I knew I could have been like that. I could have fallen in love too. To be in the choir with my colleagues. To hold their hand and cry with them at the final song "Years of high school". Despite the emotions that oppressed me, I did not give up and remained upright, trying to see my goals. I knew that I had worked too hard with myself and my psyche to give in to a situation that no one could change anyway.

When I graduated from high school, I missed Mrs Ani most, the teacher who taught me maths. She was the person who understood me best. She was the sort of truly good person one rarely meets, and her finest qualities were her gentleness and calm. I never saw her nervous in three years. She was the sort of person who could understand any situation and could see it from the other person's perspective. She knew how demanding it was for me to learn maths with only my eyes. She came twice a week for tutoring. I even spoke with her on the phone once, even though it was past ten p.m., so that she could explain an exercise to me. Not many would do what Mrs Ani did for me. I began studying under her in the tenth grade, and benefitted not only from her teaching

but also from her kindness. On Monday evening, two days before
the maths test for the baccalaureate, when she got up from the
table where we were both sitting, tears welled up in my eyes.

'You're almost done, Andreea. Good luck, my dear, I know you
can do it, I have great confidence in you.' she told me in a warm
voice, which was the way she always spoke.

I passed the baccalaureate tests with good grades, but my
plan of going to study medicine remained only in my soul. It
will always be that unfulfilled dream. But if I were to recover
tomorrow, get well and start walking, I would go to study
medicine the next day. After the many barriers that The University
of Medicine in Iaşi presented to me, I had finally found the "right
man", someone who broke down those barriers, but it was a little
too late. Initially, due to my disability the management did not
want to receive me. I couldn't go to the simulation tests either and
I was discouraged. I thought I didn't have a chance of taking the
exam. After the right person had put in a good word in for me
and after several insistences, I was allowed to take the exam. But
the confirmation came only a few days before the test. Even when
we submitted the enrolment file, I encountered difficulties.

I did not get a high enough score to take one of the places
provided by the faculty. My grade was above the minimum
required, but not enough to secure a place. I studied how
and with whom I could. I did not benefit from teachers with
experience in medical tuition. I inadvertently missed a few
answers. I had initially given the correct answer to three of them
and then I changed my mind, but I don't apologise. Maybe that's
how it was. In those moments, I angrily asked God why He would
not let me be happy, and He later showed me that happiness
does not necessarily come from the things we think we want.
Happiness comes from the things we discover over time and that
fit us without too much effort. For a while I was convinced that

I would pass the exam next year, but I thought better of it and I came to understand that sometimes it is good to know how to lose and when to stop; to know how to recognise your limits, even if it's not pleasant, and to choose the best option, even if it's not what you really want.

When I applied to do medicine, I also applied to do psychology, in Iași, where I am a student today. I knew that psychology also attracted me and it was my second choice. It's great to find out how the human psyche works and to be able to play with it, being the one in control. It's great to see that words spoken in a certain order can change a person for the better. Although it was not what I wanted with all my heart, I found myself interested in psychology more than I thought, and I want to do for people what Mrs Laura, my psychologist, did for me and many others.

44

Atypic beauty

Summer passed very slowly and was hard, as all holidays are for me. I read, I wrote, I binged on Netflix, but I also had enough time for my emotions to overwhelm me. Emotions caused by loneliness and the repeated thought that my life was simple and boring. Emotions caused by the fact that I don't have friends, I don't have someone to walk with me and encourage me. Emotions that almost made me cry and lose my mental balance. I spent more time indoors than outdoors and waited for time to pass; it was the only thing I could do. Mara visited me a few times and was vital to my recovery.

During that period we spent five days at the Golden Sands in Bulgaria. It was my first vacation with the extended family. The first vacation that wasn't just me and my parents. It's more enjoyable to go somewhere with a larger group. It was the second time that I saw the sea and the first time with my parents. I had been to the seaside once before in 2013, when I went to Eforie Sud with the dance ensemble for a festival. This time, I could not enjoy the same things as in 2013. I could not sense that pleasant feeling you have when you step on the hot sand or when the waves of the sea embrace your body. It was a different experience, but one that I enjoyed despite the shortcomings. I was glad I could see new places and I was surrounded by the extended family.

Starting in mid-September, my life returned to the rhythm I was used to before the holidays. A new edition of Atypic Beauty took place, this time in Timişoara, in Iulius Mall. On this occasion I strolled for two evenings through the old centre of Sibiu and some new streets in Timisoara. The end of October brought me to Bucharest for the annual Atypic Beauty gala, held at the Palace of Parliament and presented by Andreea Marin. There were over 1000 people and an extraordinary atmosphere. Of course, Mrs Laura and other people dear to my soul from Robănescu Hospital came to see me. It is a wonderful project and I am very happy to be part of it. At every event I am introduced to some extremely strong people, a quality that characterises the whole Atypic Beauty family, and makes me reanalyse and discover my beauty.

Following these events, I began to focus on college, and it was during this period that I was offered a new opportunity. This opportunity came as a result of Andreea Martin posting the picture from the gala on her Facebook. This makes me thank Magda Coman once again for giving me the chance to be a model in the events and thus make myself known. After the appearance of those pictures, Mrs Mărioara, a woman with an impressive story, looked me up. I knew about her, and I was already grateful to her because a year after the accident, when I was looking for a new physiotherapist, she sent Silviu, the therapist who worked in the centre she runs, to my home. Mrs Mărioara had a child who became ill at the age of nine from a rare condition and lost the fight with life at the age of fourteen. The suffering, but especially the love for her son, inspired Mrs Mărioara to open a private recovery centre for children and young people in Bacău.

We spoke on the phone and she overwhelmed me with appreciation and good thoughts (as she does every time we talk), then we met at the Daniel Centre, her centre. I met her daughter-in-law, Alina, who is on the team at the centre. It is not a very large team, but it is big enough to cover the needs of the children who come there daily. All the employees at the centre are extremely dedicated because, as Mrs Mărioara says, they do not see their job as just a job, but as a mission.

We met, we exchanged opinions, and she invited me to be a co-presenter at the awards gala for the "Star among the stars" music festival, organised by the Daniel Centre. It was a tradition for the public of Bacău and beyond. A pop music festival attended by dozens of children from several counties and popularised by well-known and appreciated artists. I accepted the proposal immediately, and I even offered to write the presentation. The gala took place at the end of November and was dedicated to the International Day of People with Disabilities, which is December 3rd. It was a unique experience for me, and for the public, who I am sure had never attended a gala presented by a person in a wheelchair. If during the first minutes the spectators looked at me strangely, I am convinced that by the end they had understood the message that I was there to impart. I am sure they understood that a strong will can overcome the impossible. I am so grateful for that experience and I would repeat it a thousand times, and for that and not only that, I thank Mrs Mărioara very much.

45

My Parents

My parents are the people behind me. They are my hands and feet, and what I am today is due to their strength. Without them, I am nothing. They are my independence, my soul, my heart, my joy, EVERYTHING. No matter how hard it was for them, they never backed down and gave up. I have encountered many cases similar to mine, cases in which the parents separated after suffering affected their lives. Well, mine always stayed together and stood up for each other.

My mother is a complicated person, but she is also very devoted and committed. She is the person who gave up her job and her personal life to take care of me 24/7. She is the person who knows every particle of my body. The person who treated my wounds with great love. The person who feeds, washes and dresses me. She combs my hair and puts on my make-up. She is the person who fulfils all my cravings and responds affirmatively to my challenges. She is extremely sensitive, and impulsive. She is a wonderful mother, caring, loving and hardworking. In the moments of utter exhaustion, she can have some outbursts that make me look at her as a different person, but I know that her good parts are above those outbursts. I know that what she does for me is very demanding and tiring and it is normal to be frustrated.

My father is the most upright man I know. He has a wonderful soul and is the man who always gives me the best advice. He is the man who told me on the hardest morning of my life that I would never die. He is a man of extraordinary kindness and perfect calm. He is a diligent father who washes, cooks, dries clothes, vacuums and much more. Gratitude, respect and generosity are other qualities that characterise him. He is an exemplary father, the type of father that not many are lucky enough to have.

My parents are the ones who care for me, turn me in bed from side to side, take me from the bed to the wheelchair and vice versa, put me in the bathtub to bathe me, lift me tens of meters to get to the places where I want to be. They do everything for me. Of course, there are also occasions when we argue and fling harsh words at each other, but the important thing is that we always come back together and know that we love each other. I wish they had a better life. I would like to give them some alone time to spend at least a few days just the two of them. I wish I could do something for them that would put a smile on their faces and make them happier. They are the only people I love with all my being, and it hurts me to know that their lives have changed because of me, because of an action I committed without thinking it through. I thank them and I am grateful for absolutely everything and I hope that one day I will make them proud of me.

46

Living in gratitude

The winter holidays passed at the same pace as every other winter holiday. They passed just as monotonously and in the same oppressive loneliness. In fact, it was the first year that no one came to sing carols to me, not even the neighbours' children. One day we met with relatives and ate together, and another day we were the host. Otherwise, everything was as normal.

The day we met my relatives for dinner, we went to my uncle and aunt. I hadn't been there since two days before the accident, when we had all gathered to celebrate Uncle's birthday. It was very overwhelming to be back there after so long. They live on the ninth floor, and the elevator is very narrow and until then none of my wheelchairs could fit in the elevator. When I entered the apartment, I almost started to cry, but I controlled myself. Every corner held a memory. I saw pictures from when I was little, from when I used to come to visit. I also recalled memories from the last day that I had walked through those rooms. I was glad to have the opportunity to remember those moments.

Someone said that memories are reversible journeys of the soul. They really are. I remember that shortly after the accident I wished I had hit my head and forgotten everything – who I was and what I am. I was wrong. Memories are among life's most precious gifts. Thanks to them, I can see faces dear to my soul, and faces of people who have long since left to please the angels.

I can see my granddad again, who made me a swing in the tree every summer – surely he made one for the angels too. Grandad was a very handsome man, both outside and inside. His eyes were blue, and his smile was contagious. He never refused me and always pleasantly surprised me.

Thanks to my memories, I can return to the places where I felt best. I can go back to moments that made me feel good. Sometimes I also revisit the bad times in my life. The soul misses a person, an image or a state of being every day. I also accumulate other feelings every day, which will always remain in my house. The soul loves to return to the moments when it met other souls too. Especially the beautiful ones. I understood that in the end our whole life will be just a memory. With good, with bad, with upsets, shortcomings and joys.

The year 2020 started very promisingly. I passed the exams of the first session in college, then there was another opportunity to keep me busy. I became the coordinator for the socialisation/integration of a support group for young people, with and without disabilities, which takes place at the Daniel Centre. It was an opportunity to meet different young people and to help with their personal development plans, but also an opportunity to gain experience in my training as a psychologist.

On 7th March, an event for Atypic Beauty took place, in Iaşi. It was dedicated to International Women's Day. We were glad to see each other again and we made plans for the next event. The social group began to take shape and to develop beautifully, bringing together different young people, until the entire planet was hit by the coronavirus pandemic, and it seemed as if everything stopped. At first it seemed like a joke, but what was happening around our country and gradually everywhere, made it a very cruel reality.

Measures were taken and strict rules imposed to try to defeat this virus. For me things were not very different compared to how I lived before the pandemic. I used to spend most of my days at home away from people anyway. However, it seemed to me that there was too much dramatization and victimisation being expressed by society. People who saw staying at home as a great tragedy. People who have no idea that what for them in those moments seemed like hell, is for others the norm, a permanent way of life. People who don't realise how lucky they are. There are hundreds of thousands of people who spend years between four walls, sitting in a bed and not being able to reach out into the outside world.

Real problems are unknown, and only a few people can imagine them. Having to follow some rules for the sake of your own health cannot be seen as a real problem. To have nowhere to sleep at night, to have nothing to eat or wear, to depend all your life on a damn device or treatment, to sit in fear next to a person who is about to lose his life, to sit in a bed with your eyes on the ceiling for months or years, to not be able to say how and what hurts, to stay in a body that no longer listens to you, these are problems, and the list could go on. Always be happy and grateful even for being able to put a cup of water to your mouth; others do not have this privilege.

Epilogue

Monday, 4th May, 2020

I have finished laying down these lines that are based on fragments of my life. I end with the same thought I started with, that willpower and ambition can make the impossible possible. I've been through a lot, maybe too much, for one person less than twenty years old. I went through a long period of denial and I was overcome with revolt, anxiety and dissatisfaction. I endured pains and sensations that I had never felt before, and some of them will be with me permanently, there being no cure to alleviate my suffering – "The only solution is to get used to the pain". I have gathered dozens of scars on my body, and some of my bones and tendons are deformed.

My whole body has changed. I have a permanent urinary tract infection due to the drainage and I can get a kidney blockage at any time. I must not get a cold because my respiratory muscles have been affected and I can't cough. Since the accident, I've only caught serious colds twice, but these times were enough that I remember every horrible sensation I was forced to endure. If I catch a cold, I have to be aspirated, otherwise I will suffocate.

It's been six years since the start of this different life. Six years of needing someone else to do everything for me. Sometimes I am so fed up with having to accept that I must be fed and washed, but I know that this is the only possible option and I can only swallow my sorrow. From an outgoing and social person, I became a person with so little social activity that I can make a short list of all the times I have been out or met people. The car accident I went through blackened my soul and showed me how much pain a person is able to accumulate.

I have never accepted what happened to me and I will never accept it. But I survived with dignity. I chose to fight side-by-side with the pain and not to limit myself. I have the pain, I live with it, but it can't have me.

There is not a day that does not hurt my soul, but I try to alleviate my suffering by looking ahead, even if most of the time this is hard for me and I feel underestimated. Even though my body remains inert, and I can only move some of my right arm, I am a student of psychology, a beauty model in a concept for the soul and the coordinator of a social group for young people with and without disabilities.

I have been judged, marginalised, excluded, discriminated against and humiliated because of my physical disability. Many have tried to stop me, to make me give up, and have made it clear to me that my place is in a bed, not among people. However, I will continue to show them what I am capable of and that my inner strength is stronger than their preconceived ideas.

I have accumulated feelings that have built my patience and strength, and I look around me with a different mentality compared to six years ago. Albert Einstein said: "There are two ways to live your life: one, as if there were no miracles and another, as if everything were a miracle". Until I became dependent on the wheelchair, I lived by the first principle. Now, I understand that everything around us is a miracle. Every gesture is a miracle. Every kind thought, every person in our life, every word, every joy, everything is a miracle. A miracle sent by God.

I did not write these tens of thousands of words to victimise or praise myself, I wrote them as an appeal. An appeal to open up and not judge before you know what is hidden behind a person. An appeal not to underestimate and marginalise. The human mind stands above physical appearance. If you take care of it, the mind remains there very capable until the last moment, but the body is transitory. Let's believe that all people are valuable, that's the principle of life.

These words are also intended for all those who have felt pain far too deeply, those marked by pain who do not hope for a second chance. From everything I have lived through, I understood that life does not stop after a tragedy, after a storm that shakes our very existence. Life goes on independently of us. But, sooner or later, sunlight appears even for the least fortunate. That's what I experienced, and I know what I'm saying. It's just that until you're in full sunshine you have to pull yourself together. Set goals, even desires. It doesn't matter if they seem impossible. Human power is above many limits, it is important to try and not to give up after the first failure. Not even after the second or tenth. Don't waste your life crying and don't consume all your energy trying to reverse something you know for sure is irreversible. Make your existence matter and be proud of yourself and your actions. Don't think about what you have lost but make what you have left important and meaningful. And don't forget, you are never in complete loneliness, God is always with you.

If you want it, you can bring happiness into your life, and your wishes can come true.

Postscript letters

Dear God,

I know that surviving the accident was a miracle on your part. I know that others who have suffered traumas like mine have died instantly. I also know that others have become dependent on a device that helps them breathe. I also know that You have a mission for every person on this earth. Please help me find mine.

You know what I've been through. You know that I did not have a very beautiful adolescence and I will probably never have the experiences that characterise a natural adult life. I will never know what it's like to fall in love and start a family. You also know how much I miss hugging my parents with my hands and dancing. You also know that I never scolded You for what you gave me to take, even though I shouted at You asking You a million times "Why me?".

You have answered my prayers many times, and for that I thank you and I am grateful to You. I asked You to take care of my parents, You have. Of course, there were situations when my family was not well, but You helped them recover. I asked You to give me a bigger space to live, You gave it to me. I asked You to give me activities to keep my mind busy, You gave them to me. I asked You to bring me a British cat, I have it, and not just any cat. These many prayers and others have been granted through the actions of people. People sent by You.

Next, please take care of my parents and never take them away from me, and if You do, take me too. I also ask You to give me at least one day to walk and enjoy everything around me before the end of my life. Let it be in reality, please, not in a dream. Ah, and thank You for those beautiful dreams when I can walk and I'm so happy, it helps me a lot, so You know.

With love, A grateful person

Dear Parents,

This is certainly not the life you wished for, and I am not the perfect child either. I'm sorry you had to go through so much suffering for my sake and you couldn't be happy like the other parents. I am sorry that you will never become in-laws and grandparents, nor will you have any of the other natural moments in the parent-child relationship. If I had a superpower, I would go back in time to do things differently and give you all the happiness in the world.

I love you; I respect you, I am grateful to you and I thank you for everything you do for me. Thank you for not giving up on me, not even for a second, for not letting me down and for not judging me, and for each time you overwhelmed me with so much love. You have given me all that you have and put my happiness above all else.

I wish I could somehow reward you for all your efforts and make your heart rejoice. I know you are physically and mentally tired, and I wish I could do something about it and stop this story. But all I can do is be proud of you, because you are the best and strongest parents in the universe, and I promise you that I will always try to make you proud of me.

With love, Your child

Dear reader,

Be kind to everyone and in any situation, even to those who have wronged you. Love and give whenever you have the opportunity. Forgive even the darkest deeds. Give thanks for everything that helps you not to cry. Recognise when you are wrong and apologise. Believe and hope until the last moment. Appreciate every moment or word that does not make you sad. Rejoice. Smile. Learn the beauty of small things. Have courage and fulfil all your dreams. Have respect for those around you. Learn how to lose. Learn how to stop something that doesn't do you any good. Be grateful. Be happy that you can see, feel, hear, get out of bed and do whatever you like.

Never give up on something you find too difficult if you have support and you know you do it wholeheartedly. Do not judge at first sight but be patient and explore. Do not forget. Don't cry and waste yourself in vain when you know that nothing more can be done.

Understand that money cannot replace health, nor can material things replace happiness. Understand that you are mortal and you cannot play with life the way you want. You are transient and you do not know for how long you will be here. Understand that boldness and arrogance do not make you a more interesting person. Understand how fragile you are and that you do not always have control over the things you are sure of.

And finally, be happy. Especially because you live, you don't just exist.

Sincerely, A person who understood these things too late